HISTORY THE BETRAYER
A study in bias

'Writing History is as important as making History. If the man who writes History is unfaithful to the man who makes it, Truth is betrayed, and Mankind pays the penalty.'

Kemal Atatürk

'. . . historians, to whom is vouchsafed the power, denied to Almighty God, of altering the past.'

Dean Inge

HISTORY
THE BETRAYER

A study in bias

E. H. DANCE

HUTCHINSON OF LONDON

HUTCHINSON & CO. (*Publishers*) LTD
178–202 Great Portland Street, London, W.1

London Melbourne Sydney
Auckland Bombay Toronto
Johannesburg New York

First published 1960

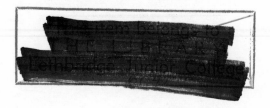

© E. H. Dance 1960

*This book has been set in Fournier type face. It has
been printed in Great Britain by The Anchor Press,
Ltd., in Tiptree, Essex, on Antique Wove paper
and bound by Taylor Garnett Evans & Co., Ltd.,
in Watford, Herts*

Contents

History or Truth?

IT IS commonly supposed that history is over and done with, and therefore unalterable. The basis of this idea is that history is the past. But history is not the past—it is the record of the past. If there is no record, there is no history; if there is a record, it has a recorder, whose views and prejudices enter into his record, and colour it. There has been much talk of 'objective' history—especially in Germany, where the word *objektiv*, rolled round the Teutonic tongue, often conveys an altogether false feeling of security. In fact, there can be no such thing as objective history. Historians (honest or dishonest) are no more objective than witnesses (honest or dishonest) in a law-court; no two of them give the same account of the same thing; and no one of them ever succeeds in saying exactly what he sets out to say about it. Stevenson's advice *Virginibus Puerisque* is equally valid for historians: 'The difficulty of literature is not to write, but to write what you mean; not to affect your reader, but to affect him precisely as you wish.'

That is why many lovers of historical truth—more especially, perhaps, history teachers, and most especially German history teachers—have often recommended sticking to dates. Dates at least, it is said, cannot lie. But that also is untrue. Take, for example, the familiar formula, 'Battle of Hastings A.D. 1066'. It looks harmless and honest enough; yet it contains at least two mis-statements of fact and one

expression of religious prejudice. To begin with, the battle
was fought not at Hastings, but six or seven miles away; that
is why Freeman and his followers strove unsuccessfully for a
couple of generations to change its name from Hastings to
Senlac. And it was not fought in A.D. 1066, but somewhere
between 1069 and 1074; for Jesus Christ was not born, as
our calendar presupposes, in the thirty-first (or should it be
twenty-seventh?) year of the reign of Augustus, but some
time earlier—perhaps 'when Cyrenius was governor of
Syria', as St Luke says.

In all west European dating there is always this inaccuracy
of from three to eight years in the reckoning. As for religious
prejudice, why should the whole world, because it has come
under the social and economic impact of a European civilization, be saddled with a Christian system of chronology? The
anomaly is intensified by the fact that the Christian system
is wrong by those three to eight years. It is bad enough for a
world mainly non-Christian to find itself forced by circumstances to reckon by Christian years: it is even worse since
the Christian system is itself basically inaccurate.

Still, there is no better alternative available. The Greek
reckoning by Olympiads, the Roman reckoning from the
foundation of their city, had both basic starting-points more
unreliable than that of the Christian calendar. As for the
dozens of systems which have begun with the creation of the
world, they have varied in their dating of that event from
our 6984 to our 3483 B.C., even in the days when the creation
was dated precisely. The Muslims, counting from the exile
of Mahomet in our A.D. 622, are handicapped by their year
of lunar months, which none of their efforts to modify have
rendered really efficient. Attempts like those of Mussolini or
the French Revolution to begin afresh in their own times
have proved worthless because they have chosen for their
datum-line movements which have proved evanescent. As

for the peoples of the Far East, for the last two thousand or
so years of their Empire the Chinese (like the annalists of
Europe in the Middle Ages) dated by the regnal years of their
rulers; India has used a dozen different systems, the best of
which is far from satisfactory. Nevertheless, all these, and
many others equally inaccurate, have been employed from
time to time, and have to be translated by European historians into our own calendar which is itself hardly less
inaccurate.

The inaccuracy of the Christian system is, however,
microscopic when compared with that of some others. The
chronology of early Egypt, for example, is based upon complicated correlations between astronomical cycles and non-
Egyptian events which can be dated with tolerable certainty.
But the year is not, after all, 365 days long, as the Egyptians
supposed, but about $365\frac{1}{4}$, so that every four years the Egyptian calendar became approximately a day out of step, and
it took 1461 ($4 \times 365\frac{1}{4}$) years to right itself. Consequently,
for some time during the present century Egyptologists were
divided into two rival schools, dating a good deal of Egyptian
history 1461 years differently from one another. There have
been similar though smaller variations for other periods.
Hammurabi, for instance, has been pushed about by the
accumulations of recent research until his reign is now put
about two hundred years earlier than it was a generation ago.
And there is the notorious case of our own Alfred the Great.
In the nineteenth century everybody dated his death at 901,
and a grand celebration was prepared for his millenary.
Before the great day, however, someone discovered that
there was a mistake; he had died, after all, in 899 or 900. So
the celebrations had to be cancelled, and the history books
came into line—though it is still said to be safest for the
cautious historian to hedge a little about 899 and 900. As
for Shakespeare, how many top-hatted and rose-bedecked

worshippers at Stratford on April 23rd realize that in fact no-body knows what Shakespeare's birthday was? The whole business is complicated by the variation between the Old Style and the New Style of the Christian calendar. This, as everyone knows, was over a week out before Pope Gregory XIII reformed it in 1582, and eleven days out when Britain adopted the reform in 1751; it still hampers communications between eastern and western Europe; and it confounds unwary students with such anomalies as the *Eikon Basilike*, which bears the imprint 1648 although it purports to give the last words of Charles I just before he was executed in what we call 1649.

If there is plenty of room for the play of personal preferences in the case of individual dates, the trouble is greatly increased when the dates are combined into lists. People who are worried about the bias in history books sometimes speak as though the Gordian knot could be cut if all the books were reduced to chronological tables. The inference is that chronological tables, which appear to consist of facts and nothing else, are bound to be free from bias. But of course that is absurd. One of the easiest ways of telling an untruth is to speak nothing but the truth—with something vital omitted. Not even the most detailed list of dates, though it may tell the truth and nothing but the truth, can possibly tell the whole truth. And what is left out can make all the difference between impartiality and prejudice. Here, for example, are two date-lists for the first quarter of the sixteenth century. They are taken from two elementary school-books, one a nineteenth-century English book, the other used in western Germany in the 1950's:

| 1510 | Execution of Dudley and Empson |
| 1512 | War with France; French fleet destroyed near Brest |

1513	Battle of Spurs; French defeated
	James IV of Scotland invaded England; defeated and slain at Flodden
1514	Peace concluded with France and Scotland
1515	Wolsey made Cardinal by the Pope, and Chancellor by Henry VIII
1518	Wolsey made Papal Legate
1520	Field of the Cloth of Gold
1521	Henry received the title of Defender of the Faith from the Pope

*   *   *

c. 1500	Italian Renaissance at its height
1483–1546	Martin Luther
1517	Luther's Theses at Wittenberg
1519–22	First circumnavigation of the world (Magellan)
c. 1520	Scientific and artistic development in Germany at its height
1524–5	Peasants' War in Germany

Each of these lists attempts to give school children the 'most important' events from 1500 to 1525; yet they have not a single item in common, because they are compiled from two different points of view—points of view which must inevitably be imparted to the pupils using them. Readers of the first are asked to interest themselves exclusively in politics and war; they will receive the impression that Englishmen fight (or fought) better than Frenchmen or Scots; and they will learn nothing whatever about world-shaking events abroad at that time, though they do learn about comparatively trivial events in England. The German list gives its pupils no information about English history, nor about anything purely political or military anywhere; it does not even mention the Battle of Pavia, which was surely one of the most significant events in German history. The whole list breathes and inculcates the escapism of a generation of war-weary German teachers. Neither list contains a word of prejudice; both lists are full of it.

The capacity of plain date-lists to be thoroughly tendentious can be seen more clearly still if this West German list is compared with another—contemporary, but from that part of Germany which is called the Soviet Zone by West Europeans, but by East Europeans the Democratic Zone:

c. 1500	Decline of the Hansa
	Beginnings of manufacture in Germany
1510	Peter Henlein constructs the first pocket-watch
1514	'Poor Conrad' Revolt
1516	Portuguese ships at Canton
	More's *Utopia*
1517	Luther's Theses
1519–21	Cortes' Conquest of Mexico
1519–22	Circumnavigation of the world by Magellan
1519–56	Emperor Charles V
1520	Beginnings of the Reformation in Switzerland (Zwingli and Calvin)
	Revolt of the Cummuneros
1521	Luther before the Diet at Worms
1524	Beginning of the Peasants' Revolt
	Muntzer's Articles
	Death of Holbein
1525	Peasants' War in Germany
	Battle of Frankenhausen
	Baber conquers all India and founds the Moghul Empire
	Death of Jakob Fugger

Here there is nothing whatever about pure politics or war: of twenty-one dates, at least seventeen are concerned with a history which is social and economic. And although, like the other lists, it confines itself to facts and contains not one contentious item, it is typical of Marxist teaching, and it is meant for use in teaching Marxism.

Sentences and paragraphs are far more prone to prejudice than mere facts and figures. Consequently, the shift in accuracy of chronological lists—which at first sight seem wholly objective—becomes anything from misleading to wicked in history books that are meant for reading. In the chronological tables, as we have seen, it is mainly a matter of biassed selection: and so it is in the reading books. The bias is plain even in the supposedly most widely conceived books—Gibbon, or Toynbee, or Macaulay whose work, though written on a scale which would have taken him 150 years to complete, is the stock example of history seen through Whig spectacles. The shorter the book, the more rigorous the selection of facts: so that, other things being equal, the shorter the book the more it is prejudiced; and school books, being necessarily the shortest of all, are often the most tendentious of all. In some ways this has long been recognized. Academic historians have always complained that school History as a subject is unreal and unscholarly, and therefore fundamentally misleading. No doubt it is, though the charge is largely irrelevant, because school books have to be written to suit school children. If they seem too selective, the selection is educationally inevitable; at least it is less objectionable than that of a Gibbon or Macaulay or Toynbee, all of whom have written selectively in order to propagate a point of view. Academic histories can be as biassed as school histories—as anyone knows who has read academic histories on the same subject by authorities of different nations, or religions, or politics. 'We cannot write

History at all without leaving out . . .' says one of them; 'the History we read, though based on facts, is strictly speaking not factual at all, but a series of accepted judgments.'[1] In truth, 'the simplified tradition which is customarily called History'[2] is simplified in different degrees. Academic History is (perhaps) less simplified than History for schools; but both are simplified, and both are to that extent untrue.

In our days the whole world has become familiar with deliberate manipulation of history for the purposes of political propaganda. It is less frequently realized that every history book, from *The Decline and Fall* to *Little Arthur's England*, puts forward a point of view which is consciously or unconsciously biassed. Gibbon, as we know, indulged himself in a long sly dig at Christianity: but even *Little Arthur's England* retails a history which is excessively English, and which is still further doctored (from the best of motives) to make it suitable for Little Arthur. Both books have succeeded in satisfying many generations of readers without going out of print; presumably, therefore, they are not unbearably biassed with the prejudices of their own age. What of the thousands of history books at all levels which, unlike Gibbon and Little Arthur, are read avidly by one generation only to be discarded by the next because they have dated too obviously? How often in our day are the historical best-sellers of the nineteenth century picked up and read for pleasure? Macaulay is too Whig, Froude too 'popular', Seeley too imperialistic, Green not social enough for a generation which owes to him pretty well all the Social History that has been written since. All are out of fashion, because all are written from points of view which are now disparaged. And the school textbooks of yesteryear, where are they?

The histories of our own time will suffer the same fate,

[1] G. Barraclough: *History in a Changing World.*
[2] C. V. Wedgwood: *The Thirty Years' War.*

because they in their turn will offend the tastes of posterity. But their bias is not merely that of the future against the present, of the present against the past. They are also all of them permeated with prejudices against their own contemporaries. This is as true of British as of foreign books. We are familiar (or are we perhaps judging merely from hearsay, without reading the books for ourselves?) with the 'cooked' histories issued by Nazis and Fascists and Communists. But we need to remember that most of the Nazis and Fascists and Communists have regarded their books, not as cooked, but as correct. If you really believe in Nazism or Fascism or Communism your belief will inevitably colour your selection of facts for history books, and you will regard this as perfectly legitimate. Britons usually suppose themselves incapable of this sort of thing. In fact, we are as sincere in our beliefs as any other peoples, and our histories are coloured accordingly. We tend to applaud Seeley's refusal—in the interests of Imperial History—to confine his consideration to 'an island off the north-west corner of Europe', and forget that *The Expansion of England* was a work of deliberate political propaganda. To British minds the propaganda seems innocent enough—but so does the propaganda of Nazism and Fascism and Communism to sincere Nazis and Fascists and Communists. How many history books, elementary and advanced, in Britain and America, have been written by sincere democrats who believe it part of their duty to propagate the virtues of parliamentary democracy? Sometimes, indeed, our educationists are quite open about this. An American book on the teaching of history claims that in learning history 'every pupil should have a conviction of the value of democratic political processes. . . . He should be alert to the threats which always confront democratic processes, but determined to expand rather than to curtail these processes'. To the ordinary Briton or American such a view

seems wholly admirable; but if we approve this propagation
of democracy, how shall we condemn a parallel Russian
claim that 'the Modern History course is of very great
importance in the formation of a Communist world-outlook
among the pupils'? If it is right for a history teacher in the
U.S.A. to foster 'a conviction of the value of democratic
political processes', is it wrong for a teacher in the U.S.S.R.
to foster 'a Communist world-outlook', at least if both
teachers are equally honest in their beliefs?

No doubt the American teacher will say that the Russian
teacher is not honest in his belief; no doubt the Russian will
say the same of the American. That sort of reasoning leads
us nowhere. Our failure to appreciate the sincerity of people
whose ideas are opposed to our own is at the bottom of most
of the misconceptions in history books, and indeed in life
itself. It was Nietzsche who prided himself on being one of
those 'who see things the other way round': and whatever
we may think of Nietzsche's philosophy, at least it will be
conceded that there is in the world too little effort to 'see
things the other way round', to escape from the fetters of
our own customary environment—political, social, intellectual, religious—and to try to enter into other people's points
of view. The passing of nearly a century has not yet invali-
dated Matthew Arnold's plea for

'a disinterested endeavour to learn and propagate the best
that is known and thought in the world, and thus to
establish a current of fresh and true ideas. By the very
nature of things, as England is not all the world, much of
the best that is known and thought in the world cannot be
of English growth, must be foreign; by the nature of
things, again, it is just this that we are least likely to know,
while English thought is streaming in upon us from all
sides and takes excellent care that we shall not be ignorant

of its existence; the English critic, therefore, must dwell much upon foreign thought, and with particular heed on any part of it which, while significant and fruitful in itself, is for any reason specially likely to escape him.'

Is it bathetic to put alongside Matthew Arnold a Pamphlet of the Historical Association, which urges that in teaching History 'it is important to choose countries with geographical features strongly differentiated from our own . . . and with governmental peculiarities which also contrast with ours'? Till there is far more effort in every nation to slough off the chrysalis of environment, our history books will continue to repeat errors and misjudgments which have become traditional, and which seem so absurd to other peoples who are themselves the victims of quite different errors and misjudgments.

Some of these foreign errors and misjudgments can be quite astounding to Britons unfamiliar with foreign history books. It is, for example, not uncommon for Spanish children to be brought up on an account of the Armada which leaves the English out altogether. According to this version, the weather (and a certain amount of Spanish ill-luck and incompetence) was wholly to blame for disaster—such English activities as there were made little difference one way or the other. And if this seems too rich to be believed it can be paralleled by a West German account of the Crimean War, and an East German account of the war of 1939–45, both of which also omit any mention of England. To an Englishman history such as this seems midsummer madness. Yet there is something to be said for the foreign view in each case. The Spaniards can point to books of other nations, some of which seem to accept the Spanish view about the Armada, as well as to Queen Elizabeth's own Armada medal, which attributes the Spanish disaster to the weather alone. As for the English share in the last world war, it is certainly unbalanced of Communists not to teach their children about it; but lack of balance is not uncommon among foreigners (even when the foreigners are British), and Communists thinking only in terms of casualties and fighting-hours can perhaps be understood, though not excused, if they omit the English share in such statistics.

At any rate it is clear that, rightly or wrongly, all nations do look at things from their own way round, and that their history books, and especially their school history books, seem to suffer accordingly. Plenty of examples can be given from the extent of history. All peoples (not excluding ours) tend to exaggerate their own prowess in all the wars they have fought. There is the case of the English and the French in the Hundred Years' War. The bald summaries which pass muster for History in the British school-books always mention the four battles of Sluys, Crecy, Poitiers and Agincourt. The bald summaries which pass muster for History in the French school-books are quite capable of overlooking any or all of these battles, and concentrating instead on the defensive strategy of Bertrand du Guesclin, the epic of Joan of Arc, and the French victories at the end of the hundred years. The result is that English children are encouraged in a belief that Englishmen fight better than Frenchmen, and French children in a belief that Frenchmen fight better than Englishmen. It is even true that many English children find themselves frustrated when they learn that at the close of the wars not all the English victories had prevented our expulsion from France. There is a similar tale to tell of the Spanish Succession and the Napoleonic Wars. No English schoolboy is allowed to get away without learning the names and dates, and often the tactics, of Blenheim, Ramillies, Oudenarde and Malplaquet: many French books disregard all these battles, and some even omit Marlborough altogether. Few French books fail to mention the battle of Denain: it appears in hardly any English school-book. In both countries pupils are led to suppose that their own country won the war; and both are right, since it is certainly true that in the War of the Spanish Succession the Spanish Succession went to France, and that at the end of the war the English Empire was far bigger than at the beginning. As for the wars against Napoleon, in all the English school-books Trafalgar and Waterloo loom much larger than Marengo, Ulm, Austerlitz, Jena, Friedland, Borodino and Leipsic put together—not unnaturally perhaps, but certainly to the undeserved detriment of Napoleon's fame in England. And the various claims about the battle of Waterloo are almost comic. At a recent international conference of history teachers the question was put: which general deserves credit for the victory? Wellington, said the delegates from Britain, America and Italy: Blücher, said the West Germans: the French gave it first to Blücher, and secondly to Wellington: the Dane to Wellington first, then Blücher: the Austrian and Norwegian delegates to Wellington and Blücher equally. The Dutchman declined to give a reply, but the Belgian had no such scruples: Wellington certainly, he said, was in command; but the battle would have been lost if a Belgian general had not ignored Wellington's signal to retreat.

‹ It will be noticed that these conflicting points of view are due, not (as is often supposed by academic historians) to ignorance of research and scholarship, but to biassed selection among facts which are quite well known and often commonplace. The difficulty is that the commonplaces are different in different countries. Each people tends to recall and record the things which are congenial to itself, and to forget or ignore those which are favourable to foreigners. What is lacking in all countries is the will to see things the other way round, and the effort (it must inevitably be strenuous, for the fight against one's own prejudices is always hard) to think oneself out of an intellectual medium in which one has lived and thought all one's life, in order to comprehend the environment in which the foreigner has lived all his life.

'In proportion as we love truth more and victory less, we shall become anxious to know what it is which leads our opponents to think as they do. We shall begin to suspect that the pertinacity of belief exhibited by them must result from a perception of something which we have not perceived. And we shall aim to supplement the portion of truth we have found with the portion found by them.'[1]

It can be surprising what rudimentary things others may have perceived which we have not perceived. And not merely in matters of detail. The whole of history is often misrepresented because we regard it too narrowly from our own little spot on the earth's surface. Among West Europeans, for instance, all history is invariably divided into Ancient, Medieval and Modern. 'Ancient' means, roughly, to the end of the Roman Empire: 'Modern' means, roughly, since about the time of the Renaissance: 'Medieval' means the time between. But not only is the term 'Modern History' becoming more and more meaningless as 'modern times' extend further from the seventeenth century, when the label 'Middle Ages' was invented: the very conception of a Middle Age (or Middle Ages, as the English alone call it) has no validity outside western Europe. Beyond the Oder there was no Renaissance, no Roman Empire, and therefore no medieval times; in the lands of the former Byzantine Empire the Middle Age has no beginning, though perhaps it ends in 1453; everywhere in Europe east of the Elbe 'modern times' are now reckoned as beginning, not with the Renaissance, but

[1] Herbert Spencer: *First Principles*.

in the middle of the seventeenth century: while throughout Asia and Africa all history needs redividing into fresh periods wholly unknown to the West.

In Communist countries this is already being done. The two principal Communist countries, Russia and China, are among those which had no Middle Ages in our sense, and in Communist Europe, at least, historians have begun to jettison the Middle Ages altogether. The tendency there is to divide history into two periods instead of three; and (surprisingly enough to us of the conservative West) the dividing line they choose is the English Civil War. The reason usually given is that the English Civil War transferred the control of government from the nobility to the middle classes, and ushered in that communist equivalent of the Middle Ages: the period of transition between aristocracy and communist democracy. But in fact there are plenty of non-communist reasons for adopting this chronological arrangement. In the last generation or two, our own western historians have been deposing the Renaissance and Reformation from their once proud position as the onset of modern times. The Reformation, they say, was an end and not a beginning; as for the Renaissance, some of them deny that there ever was one. About 1650, on the other hand, not only did an English Parliament kill an English king and shackle his successors, but in addition, the continental peace settlement of 1648–59 put an end to the Hapsburg dream of European supremacy and replaced it by that of France, saw the beginnings of Prussianism, recognized Switzerland and Holland for the first time, and marked the temporary extinction of Germany. Beyond the political plane, in 1642, Galileo died and Newton was born; Bacon had already ensured that, in future, science was to be experimental and not merely speculative; scientific academies were developing all over Europe; so were factories; and across the Atlantic, colonialism was already a rising concern. It was the seventeenth century which saw the end of the Mediterranean Age and the clear emergence of the Age of the Atlantic.

In other words, from the seventeenth century onwards, the subject matter of history ought to have included entirely new topics. It ought to have included them, but it did not. The historians of the seventeenth, eighteenth and nineteenth centuries barely strayed from the political paths of their predecessors. There is little but politics in Clarendon or Bossuet or Voltaire or Gibbon or Hume or Macaulay—or even Ranke. Only with Marx did the economic side of history receive due recognition. Not even yet do our histories pay a fair share of attention to science and industry (including the Industrial Revolution in farming) which, with the basic factors of the family and society, have made the modern world what it is.

Even on the merely political plane the histories are still hopelessly unbalanced. If it was proper for the historians of the past to show their democratic readers how they had become democratic, it is even more important for the historians of the present to make clear the evolution of our increasingly international society. Yet how many of our school books so much as mention the name of Grotius? And how many even of the academic histories of Europe devote a single page to the evolution of the European idea in the minds of the men who followed Grotius—Penn, St. Pierre, Vattel, Bentham, Kant, Victor Hugo and the rest?

All this is as true of the areas as of the periods covered by our history books. Most of them have been written and published west of the Oder and Danube; and consequently, have given short shrift to the countries east of the Oder and Danube. Even the academic histories say far too little about Byzantium, Poland and Turkey; the school-books ignore them almost completely, except for the periods when they

have been the victims of western attacks. Naturally, therefore, educated Europeans are often quite ignorant about
the elements of greatness in Byzantine, and still more in
Polish and Turkish history. Ask any ten history graduates
of British universities which was the largest state in Europe
in the sixteenth century; nearly all of them will get the
answer wrong. And beyond eastern Europe lies a whole
Orient of mighty peoples with an incomparable past about
which western Europeans know nothing at all. It is in the
East that most of the civilizations of the world have been
born and flourished; yet the essential parts of the history of
them all remains a closed book to nearly everybody in
Europe and America. And not only to these; the eastern
peoples themselves are ignorant of their own history. Most
of the East has never been given to historiography; materials
for a history of the East comparable to those for histories of
the West do not exist—cannot exist until after generations
of patient scholarship and research. European orientalists say
that there is not a single good history of China in any European language. Something similar is said about Indian history
by most Indian historians of Indian nationality.

In other words, history as known to Europeans is completely unbalanced. It is unbalanced partly because, as we
have seen, the history of most of the world has not been
written, and cannot be written yet—perhaps ever. Even what
has been written is unbalanced, because it is conventional to
deal with only a few areas which are of immediate interest,
and to discount the history of those areas which used to be
far away from Europe and the West—though modern communications have brought them into the same political and
cultural orbit. It was this which moved the great French
orientalist Grousset to cast up his *Balance Sheet of History*,
in which Asia occupies about half the credit side—not a
tenth or a hundredth, as in most of our western histories.

Conventional limitations of our history are not merely local; they are topical and intellectual as well. Our own generation has been warned to beware of the Whig interpretation of history, biassed by the idea that the be-all and end-all of human evolution is parliamentary democracy. The Whig interpretation, however, is only one of many unbalanced interpretations of history with which our books trouble to make us familiar. There is a Tory interpretation of history as well; it tends to run to Imperialism. Disraeli began it in the grand style over a century ago, and it has since passed through the hands of Seeley and Kipling and Fletcher into the hands of equally eminent historians of our own day. Imperialism (British Imperialism at any rate) has been obsessed with the white man's burden, and with the corollary conception of the historical unworthiness of races which are 'coloured'. Most of the people of the world are 'coloured'; not more than four of Toynbee's twenty-odd civilizations have been the work of the unpigmented peoples of the West. Yet there are no world histories in any language which give one-fifth, let alone the just four-fifths, of their space to these great 'coloured' civilizations, living and dead. Indeed, there are still, in Europe and America, millions of educated people capable of regarding these civilizations as unreal, and their makers as no better than barbarians. In our conception of 'barbarism', as in so much else, we are true children of the Hellenes.

Beyond colour and race, there is religion. The world has seen more religions even than civilizations; four or five of the greatest of them are still flourishing. All of them are oriental in origin. But because only one of them migrated westward and changed Europe into Christendom, it alone gets fair treatment in the schools of Europe and America. School history books, elementary and advanced, are full of Christian churches and councils and popes and schisms and reformations; bishops, priests and deacons (monastic and other) move conspicuously across their pages; sometimes, even, the history books mention Christian doctrine. But neither the teachings nor the organization of the other religions receive in the textbooks anything more than a superficial and usually condescending glance, so that our schoolchildren grow into citizens lamentably ignorant of the moral and spiritual treasures which the non-Christian religions have to offer.

They say that Herodotus was the Father of History. As he moved about on his travels he wrote down what he happened to learn about the places which happened to interest him. Sometimes (if he became deeply interested) he wrote a good deal about them. About the places which failed to arrest his sympathies he wrote little or nothing at all. The history served up to us today bears every mark of the paternity of Herodotus.

2

Clio Bemused

ONE of the most frequent misconceptions about bias in history is that the real remedy is for researchers to push ahead diligently with their researches until they have succeeded between them in establishing 'the truth'. After that the only thing necessary is for the writers of textbooks to put 'the truth' into textbooks. It is an attractive theory—attractive especially to the archivists, who know what nonsense is often written by historians less familiar than themselves with the archives. Like a good many other attractive theories, however, it is ludicrously untrustworthy. In the first place, it may take anything from years to generations for the discoveries of research to percolate into the school-books. And for this the textbook writers are not to blame. Articles on research are legion; they deal with all history from before Adam till after Hitler and no textbook writer can keep pace with a hundredth of them. For another thing most specialist research is published in journals which few textbook writers can be expected to see—and in any case many a new piece of research is followed by another, contradictory piece of research, in some equally inaccessible publication. Eventually 'the truth' gets into the major histories, and from there it reaches the school-books; by which time it is quite likely that 'the truth' has become an 'interpretation of history' which the academies have decided to discard.

Secondly, there is the uncomfortable fact which we all know, though we all have to disregard it in practice, that 'the truth' itself is elusive. The philosophers (who are as competent in their line as the archivists in theirs) have no hesitation in assuring us that, wherever or however we seek, the truth will escape us—like Wellington telling his contemporaries not to try to write accounts of what happened at Waterloo, because he didn't know himself and was sure they never would, either. Historical 'truth' is as elusive as any other—not merely because man rarely knows the truth when he sees it, but because he is still more rarely capable of communicating it to others. For instance, if you tell a child that King John 'signed' Magna Carta the universities of Europe will shudder in unison. Yet that verbal 'untruth' will convey to a modern child, reared among business people, something much nearer the truth about Magna Carta than any sentence carefully compiled by a conscientious teacher in an attempt to explain what John really did to it. Once he lets his class become interested in the fascinating routine of medieval chancellaries they will concentrate on that and forget all about Clause 39, which is the chief business in hand. In any case, we all know that it is often wise to avoid telling children the truth until they are old enough to grasp it—in history teaching, no less than the broader facts of life. Good teachers select their facts to suit the capacities of the pupils with whom they are dealing at the moment. Hardly any pupil of secondary age can possibly understand, for instance, the implications of the South Sea Bubble, and therefore the less said to children about it the better—or about Walpole's political methods, which it would be good for children not to know, even if they could understand them. The same is true of many other things which at present are put blindly into the curriculum.

This is not to deny that there are historical matters, in

both teaching and textbook, on which research can often shed a necessary light. British, French, German, Russian historians differ fundamentally about the causes of wars in which they have fought one another, largely because each side is ignorant of the archives of the others, and sometimes of its own. Until the Foreign Offices release their documents more willingly, especially for recent times, the historians cannot possibly complete their picture. Besides, so long as historians can read their own languages better than foreign ones, they will remain more familiar on the whole with their own side than with the other in any disputed question.

English historians, for example, usually read English better than German and German better than Danish. No wonder the Danes are always complaining that in English accounts of the Schleswig-Holstein crisis of 1863–4, while Palmerston's policy is given in full, and the policies of Prussia and Austria at least discussed, the essentials of the Danish case usually go by default, because few English historians have been able to tackle the Danish documents. Similarly, Scots tend to claim that if English books were more closely based on the authorities they would cease to represent the battle of Culloden as an English victory, and instead describe it accurately as a victory of Britons over Britons. Americans assert that nearly all European historians betray ignorance of the earlier events of the Industrial Revolution in the United States. Germans ask foreign historians to look more closely into the population and cultural statistics of Alsace before they decide that it is naturally French. From Holland comes the charge that British accounts of the acquisition of Cape Colony always suppress essential considerations favouring its retention by the Dutch. And quite apart from specific complaints of these kinds, there always lurk behind the corner those yet undiscovered facts which are bound to upset our established notions as soon as research has managed to unearth them.

It seems natural to begin with the differences between English and German teachers about one another's history, partly because England and Germany have been at logger-heads for so long, and partly because there is more evidence available about Anglo-German textbook criticism than about any other. During the past few years the young International Schoolbook Institute at Brunswick has been exchanging text-books and criticisms with twenty or more other countries ranging round the globe, and England was the first country to co-operate with the Germans in this. Thirty or forty books have been examined on each side, and all the criticisms have been published in the Institute's *International Yearbook of History Teaching*. So that by now there is no excuse for German and English history teachers not to know what they think of each other.

Of the two, the Germans certainly come better out of the investigation. This will no doubt surprise those who have read German textbooks of the Nazi time or earlier; but there is a good reason. It is not that the Germans have fewer prejudices than the British. But all the German history books in use in 1945 were destroyed in a vast Allied holocaust of Nazi teaching material. We were determined to root out the blatantly propagandist history books of the Nazi régime, and one result was that at the beginning of the Allied occu-pation German teachers and pupils found themselves with no history books at all. The Germans had to start from scratch with the writing of their history textbooks, and of course the authors wrote them with the Nazi collapse vividly present in their minds. Moreover, all the new books were subjected to an Allied censorship. Every German author and publisher knew that no book would have a chance unless it cut completely adrift from Nazi ideas. And in any case, only authors who believed in democracy could possibly write books which the occupying powers would accept. Authors with totalitarian convictions had to lie low; liberal-minded teachers had the field to themselves. In West and East Germany alike, therefore, all the new books conformed to Allied preconceptions of what history books should contain.

So it was inevitable that when Anglo-German exchanges of textbooks began, the English critics should find little to criticize. German critics, on the other hand, were dealing with English books nearly all published before the 1939–45 war, and in most cases written during the 1930's, when anti-German feeling in this country was at its height. Consequently the Germans had no difficulty in finding anti-German 'prejudice' in the English books, whereas in the German books the English critics found little more than an occasional slip or misunderstanding. Indeed, English reports on the German books sometimes go out of their way to emphasize their admirable objectivity, their freedom from anything 'calculated to offend the most sensitive Englishman or to encourage the most Anglophobe child'. 'If this,' says another English reviewer, 'and the parent book are typical of contemporary German textbooks, one can be content; if the pupils who study them should in the future turn to false gods, it will not be the fault of the history books they studied in school.'

Still, there are historical beliefs shared by all Germans, from extreme Nazis to the most sinister Communists, which many Englishmen cannot accept; and these beliefs have found their way into the new books. Some of them, of course, are about the two world wars and their causes. No German historian will admit the sole responsibility of Germany for either of these wars. (Has there ever been, throughout the whole of historiography from Thucydides to Toynbee, any major historian who has admitted the sole responsibility of his own people for any major war?) Even democratic Germans believe that their country's foes were at least partly to blame, and therefore English critics have found in the German books too little about British efforts to avoid war before either 1914 or 1939. The Belgian neutrality treaty of 1839 tends to be ignored, though it was that which brought Britain into the war in August 1914. (Incidentally, recent research even in Britain seems to show that the German chancellor could not have described that treaty as a 'scrap of paper'.) When it comes to air warfare, the Germans make much of the bombardment of their own cities, and all too little (sometimes nothing at all) of the bombing of London or Coventry. So far there is no peace settlement since 1945 for them to quarrel with; but they over-simplify the Treaty of Versailles of 1919, though they seem to avoid the Nazi practice of calling it a Diktat; and they stress the Allied acceptance of Wilson's Fourteen Points without also stressing the Allied reservations about them.

Even for earlier periods English critics found some of the German books less than satisfactory. Like every people, they have what seems to foreigners an exaggerated idea of their own importance, which leads them, for example, to treat 'Germanism' as an equivalent of Christianity and the Hellenic tradition in the formation of the European community. They tend to depict the German agricultural developments of the eighteenth and nineteenth centuries as the pioneer agricultural revolution. Too much is said about the economic and military side of British imperialism, too little about the role of religion in the foundation of the early colonies. Similarly, the abolition of slavery in the British Empire in 1833 is sometimes attributed solely to economic motives, whereas every Englishman knows that pure philanthropy played a very prominent part indeed. And one German book at least adopts the common Dutch view that Holland was 'robbed' of Cape Colony in 1815.

It is perhaps true that since the relaxation of the Allied occupation there has been some recrudescence of those more 'nationalistic' views which were current in Germany even before the Nazi times. After a decade or more of possibly too passive acquiescence, some of the books are beginning to revive ideas which are more characteristically 'German'. It is, in fact, inevitable that textbooks should reflect, and even encourage, current notions of the prevailing environment. In a Germany consciously straining towards parliamentary democracy and internationalism, democracy and internationalism will influence the history textbooks. And now that older German ideals of politics and culture are reviving, some of the history books already reflect such ideals. There is nothing 'wrong' about this. Germans are as much entitled as British or Americans or Russians to hold to, and to teach their children, the traditions they have inherited. It is hardly surprising, therefore, that one or two English critics have found in several German books ideas and attitudes prevalent not merely under the Nazis, but also during the quasi-democratic days of the Weimar Republic. One book in particular has been condemned by its English reviewer for 'exaggerated attention to military history, underlined by the choice of illustrations', and for minimizing the sufferings caused by German bombing, deportations, and atrocities generally, while making the most of those to which the Germans were subjected in their turn. 'The author's treatment of the Soviet system is one-sided and entirely negative. It should be compared with his persistent attempts to bring out the positive aspects of the National Socialist system.' And in a final sweeping summary the reviewer condemns the later part of the book as 'a disgrace to historiography and to the Federal German Republic, which must inevitably warp

the minds of school children unfortunate enough to be
brought up in the spirit of the author'.

It should be said that so far this is the only one of the
German books to receive such severe condemnation. And of
course it would be easy for the author to reply that in fact
German history cannot be written impartially without stressing its military aspects; or that he really believes German
atrocities were, in fact, greatly exaggerated by Allied propaganda; or that he regards the actions of Communist Russia
as even worse than those of Nazi Germany; or that he and
his fellow-Germans were less in the grip of poverty under
Hitler than under the Weimar Republic. Nevertheless, this
English opinion is perhaps a pointer. Possibly the democratic
and international spirit which has marked almost all the
German textbooks since 1945 is less typical of Germany as a
whole than it has appeared to be: that is a question which
will not be answered for some time yet.

No German criticism of English books is anything like
so condemnatory. On the other hand, no English book
receives from the Germans such unreserved approval as most
of the German books receive from the English. None of our
books has been described as free from anything 'calculated
to offend the most sensitive' German. Instead, the Germans
find all our books still too much under the influence of ideas
which they feel we ought by now to have outgrown. Some
of these are mere matters of detail. For example, they say as
usual that we give Wellington too much and Blücher too
little of the credit for victory at Waterloo; that we minimize
the number of Germans in Alsace, or the German characteristics of the Holy Roman Empire. We treat Austria
(especially in the nineteenth century) as though she were
not part of Germany—indeed, the most important part.
And there is the usual tale of significant omissions. Our
textbooks seem unaware of the permanent Slav peril to the

B

eastern frontiers of Germany; or of the domestic reforms of
Frederick the Great or Bismarck (the French make the same
complaint about our treatment of Napoleon). One English
book (and one which is deservedly popular) makes no mention at all of either Luther or Calvin in its account of the
Reformation. In fact, the German critics notice throughout
our books a wholly insufficient attention to all the chief
German movements in the direction of freedom. They con-
tend that there has always been a strong feeling for freedom
in Germany, though it has usually been stifled by the chances
of history. Freedom permeates the writings of Luther, as of
Lessing and Kant and Goethe and Schiller, of Fichte and
Humboldt and Heine and the Grimms and Mommssen and
Mann; and whereas young Germans are taught about the
work of all these writers, young foreigners rarely hear of
them.

This is simply one more indication that textbook writers
are too often in the grip of inert ideas. Authors of English
textbooks in the mid-twentieth century have been brought
up and have lived their adult lives in an environment which
assumes that Germany is opposed to freedom; and this idea
is projected into our attitude towards the German past.
Certainly, the German past has witnessed plenty of tyranny
and aggression; but this the British books do not overlook,
as they do overlook what one German book (by a professor
in an American University) calls 'Germany's Forgotten
Freedom'. During the eighteenth and nineteenth centuries
the German urge to freedom was particularly active—in
literature primarily, but also in politics during the War of
Liberation against Napoleon, in 1830 and 1848, in the
political parties which opposed Bismarck and William II,
and of course during the Weimar Republic. Yet textbooks
which cannot afford a sentence here or there about all these
movements will go out of their way to quote against Bismarck

his unlucky phrase about Blood and Iron—as though blood
and iron were features of none but German wars; 'for where
in the whole of History,' asks one German reviewer, 'is
there a case of an empire *not* founded by force?' Or again:
'the author (of one English book) sees the course of German
history in the nineteenth and twentieth centuries *only* from
the point of view of a German attempt at world domination';
and if any Englishman retorts that this is a true interpretation
of German history, Germans can only point in astonishment
at maps of the British and of the German empires. Again, in
the era of Palmerston and Bismarck, we seem deliberately to
whitewash the one and to blacken the other, without applying
the same standards to both. We are asked to contrast two
short passages from the same English book: 'Bismarck worked
in his way to strengthen the position of Germany. He did
this by exploiting the lower side of human nature in the interest
of Germany alone'; whereas in 1914 we British were misled
by our 'naïve belief in the innate honesty and kindness of
others which, when the terrible moment arrived, made
Asquith and Grey able to lead a horrified but united nation
into war with clean hands and a pure heart'. If this sort of
stuff nowadays merely causes the average Englishman to
smile, the reflection that it appeared in an English textbook
forty years after 1914 is more likely to cause the average
German to weep with chagrin.

These German criticisms of our treatment of the great
wars and their origins reflect a fundamental difference in
approach to the whole question of war guilt. Certainly both
in 1914 and in 1939 it was Britain which declared war on
Germany and not the other way round. The reply to that is
easy—the declarations were merely our inevitable reaction
to previous German aggression. The counter-reply is equally
easy—any aggression there was must be attributed to the
attempt of western Europe to impede Germany in its inevi-

table progress towards becoming one of the greatest of the great powers. And so the ball is tossed to and fro, and English school-books (according to the German critics) minimize the Germans' difficulties while making the most of their own.

We are accused of similar mental inertia in our treatment of the grouping of alliances before the war of 1914. British accounts of the preliminary diplomacy seem to the Germans to take too much for granted—as though Anglo-German hostility was inevitable from the beginning. German critics point out that when Germany was beginning her career as a great power England was far from alliance with France. On the contrary, France and Britain were avowed enemies in the Mediterranean and elsewhere; and there was much pro-German feeling in Britain. Queen Victoria married a German; the Kaiser's mother was English; Rhodes left his scholarships to Germans as well as to British and Americans; and so on. There was even an attempt, at the turn of the century, to form an Anglo-German alliance against France and Russia. Yet English school-books hardly ever mention this, owing to the revolution in British policy which led to the surprising *entente* with France in 1904, and the still more surprising *entente* with Russia three years later. Even William II, the Germans say, is regularly misrepresented. He was in favour of the English alliance; he did not sabotage the disarmament proposals at the Hague Conference of 1898—he merely said about them in public what the other powers were saying about them in private. In 1906 and 1911, during the Moroccan crises with France, he worked hard to maintain peace; and when war came against his will in 1914, he warned his generals of the judgement to come. Some at least of these German claims will astound British people brought up in contrary traditions, and the truth about them cannot be known until all the relevant archives have been worked through when they are made available. Meantime it will do Germans and British

alike no harm to realize that their charges against one another
are not proven.

There has, however, been at least one recent attempt
to anticipate the judgment of a better-informed posterity.
During the occupation of Germany after 1945 the British
Foreign Office, anxious to put the British view across in
Germany while the going was good, encouraged among
other things joint conferences between English and German
teachers. The Germans welcomed these conferences, because
they too had views which they were equally anxious to get
across to the British. In a large number of meetings, British
and German teachers sat round tables talking things over;
and in some of the conferences at least it turned out that there
was less difference between the two sides than had been
thought. Twice, therefore (in 1950 and 1955), such conferences tried to work out accounts of the causes of the First
World War which both sides felt able to accept. These two
drafts have since been published in both England and Germany. The first, compiled by a conference mainly of school
teachers, confined itself to the rudimentary requirements of
textbooks for schools; the second, drawn up mainly by
university teachers, was intended for the guidance of authors
of advanced textbooks. In both England and Germany they
aroused a good deal of opposition from critics unable to
abandon views which had already hardened into orthodoxy.
But at least they were honest attempts to guide authors of
textbooks through the bewildering maze of claim and counter-
claim, fact and counter-fact which makes so risky any attempt
to tell the truth simply, to school children or to university
students, about the origins of the First World War. Young
people cannot afford to be kept in ignorance about these
things until the archivists in the various countries have ceased
contradicting one another.

*   *   *

But it is clear that the main trouble about bias in the
history books has nothing at all to do with research. What is
amiss is not that historians go wrong about matters known
only to the wise and prudent, but that they are ignorant of
elementary things which have been revealed unto babes. In
England, for example, historians seem not to know what
every child in Russia knows, that Ivan IV was not called the
'Terrible', but 'Grozny', which means, not that he was more
cruel than his English contemporary Bloody Mary, but that
the Tsar of all the Russians shared with God (to whom the
epithet was more frequently applied by Russians before 1917)
a certain quality of awesome majesty. In Russia, historians
seem not to know, what every English child knows, that the
novels of Dickens are not a good guide to economic con-
ditions in modern Britain. Christian historians seem not to
know, what every English-speaking Muslim knows, that to
use the word 'Mahometan' (in any of its spellings) is to deny
the unity of God. Muslim historians cannot realize, what
every child in Christendom is taught, that although the
Father is God, the Son is God and the Holy Ghost is God,
yet they are not three gods but one God. Muslims are accused
of belief in a sensuous heaven by people who take the Book of
Revelation as seriously (or as figuratively) as a Muslim takes
the Koran. Non-British historians seem not to realize that the
size of the British Navy in the past has been due, not to a
desire to dominate, but to the strategic necessities of an island
country with a lop-sided economy. Historians of western
Europe fail to appreciate what is patent to every educated
Russian, how very land-locked Russia's ports have been
throughout her history. French historians appear unconscious
that all German history has been conditioned far more by
what happens across the Vistula than by what happens across
the Rhine. European histories (all but the most advanced)
treat the United States as a land of one culture instead of many

—and some elementary books treat it as a land of no culture at all. And so on; it would be easy to stretch the list out to the crack of doom.

This ignorance in many countries of things that are commonplaces in others extends in many different directions. It involves little things—such as the birthplace of Copernicus, whom both Germans and Poles invariably claim as one of their own nationals. It involves far bigger things, like the basic patterns of foreign cultures—for instance, the western belief that there is no religious freedom in China because the Chinese do not welcome Christian missionaries, or the Chinese belief that there is no religious freedom in the West, because westerners cannot belong to more than one religion at a time. A few years ago English public opinion was stirred to a fury of indignation against the Russians when some English soldiers who had married wives in Russia were not permitted to bring them home. The whole thing became another count in the case against Communism. Nobody in England seemed to know that it had nothing to do with Communism. No English historian explained that Russian social tradition for centuries has been dead against Russian women marrying and breeding out of their fatherland; and that three hundred years before the birth of Marx there was a quite well-known similar case, when a Danish ambassador to Moscow was refused permission (in 1515) to take his Russian bride to Denmark.

This is typical of a good deal of historical bias. It is often difficult to tell whether the prejudice is due more to accidental ignorance, or to an almost wilful refusal to learn what one would rather not know. Where any group antipathy already exists we tend to welcome fresh evidence in its favour, and to ignore fresh evidence against it. We like to think that we are right and that our opponents are wrong, and our capacity for conviction reacts accordingly. Among the peoples of the Atlantic civilization this kind of closed mind is most conspicuous in politics, because the West is more politics-conscious than the rest of the world. Thus it was not unnatural for the history writers of the United States (until they took themselves in hand fifty years ago) to read and write their inherited hatred of Britain into their accounts of British history—so that it is sometimes said that Roosevelt adopted his anti-British line at the end of the Second World War because he had read the wrong history books at school. Similarly, in the case of Alsace, French books tend to emphasize the influence of French culture, while German books tend to emphasize the influence of German language and nationality. The antipathy towards France which British opinion inherited from the eighteenth century and the time of Napoleon tends to be reflected backwards into our histories of much remoter periods—the Hundred Years' War, for instance. It is not fantastic to suggest that many English imputations of French folly at Crécy and elsewhere have been coloured as much by the caricatures of Gilray as by the *Chronicles* of Froissart.

And as usual it is a mistake to suppose that these antipathies are confined to the history of politics and war. They are equally conspicuous in the histories of science and culture—even of agriculture. English short histories of science will say that oxygen was first isolated by Priestley; continental short histories usually give the credit to Scheele. French historians of farming in the first century A.D. will call Pliny's wheel-and-coulter plough 'Gallic' (not *'française'*); German historians will call it 'Germanisch' (not *'deutsch'*). In German histories (and many others) the first scientific institute of agriculture will be that of Liebig at Giessen; in English histories (and few others) it will be that of Lawes at Rothamsted. Even the developments of our own times are not exempt. School histories describing atomic research, if

they are English, make Rutherford the big man; if they are
Scandinavian, Bohr; and at least one German book comes
down with a single definite date—'1938: Atom-splitting by
Hahn'—mentioning no one else. And so the children of the
whole world grow up with the impression that their own
people has done more for civilization than any other. In all
these cases a very little research, not among documents in
archives, but in the popular books and elementary histories of
other countries, would correct national complacencies and
prevent them accumulating, as they do, like rolling snow-
balls.

It is this kind of complacency (not, as with most of our
German critics, factual inaccuracy) of which the French tend
to accuse us. Fewer French than German criticisms of
British books have been published, but their general tenor
is clear: the English textbooks suffer from *une manifestation
d'orgueil national, conscient ou inconscient, qui minimise le rôle
de tous ceux qui ne sont pas Anglais*. As in the Hundred Years'
War and the War of the Spanish Succession we mention all
the British victories and none of the French ones (except,
sometimes, one which the French won in Spain under the
generalship of the bastard son of an English king), so in the
battle of Waterloo we give far too much credit to Wellington
and far too little to Blücher. Among the causes of the French
Revolution we exaggerate the influence of American Independence; in the Revolution itself we make too much of the
atrocities, because they were directed against our friends the
émigrés, and too little of the constructive side of the movement; we 'hero-worship' Pitt and Wellington in a manner in
which the French, they claim, do not 'hero-worship' even
Napoleon; and we praise the settlement of 1815 as keeping
Europe on the whole at peace for a century, because we ourselves had no major war, disregarding the disasters in which it
landed the Greeks and South Americans in the eighteen-

twenties, France in 1830 and 1848 as well as before and after, the Balkans in the fifties and seventies and before 1914, France and Italy and Germany from before 1848 till after 1870, and so on.

The French themselves are anything but guiltless of the most perilous complacency of all—what Nehru has called 'the curious illusion of all peoples and all nations that in some way they are a chosen race'. A very great historian, Lavisse, once wrote a very small history for primary schools. One chapter is headed 'Les Conquêtes de la France': it contains a picture of Arabs attacking some French troops in Algeria— and then, in italics, *the whole world was proud of the bravery of our soldiers*. Alongside there is a picture of a French school in Algeria, and the caption (again in italics) *France wants the little Arabs to be as well taught as little French children; that proves that our France is kind and generous to the peoples she has conquered*. One is hardly surprised to find that the very last words of this elementary history by a famous French historian, not this time in italics, but in enormous capitals, are VIVE LA FRANCE! It all sounds very foolish, forty years on, but hardly more foolish than the white man's burden with which English textbooks of forty years ago abounded. Even now, how many English textbooks avoid giving all the credit for the prosperity of modern Egypt to Cromer? How many, when they are dealing with Mehemet Ali and his relations with Palmerston, trouble to mention that it was Mehemet Ali who began the reform of Egyptian land tenure and the long progress of education, and who constructed a canal between Alexandria and the Nile? Yet these are common-places in the few histories written by Egyptians.

Everywhere the story is the same. Germans and Turks and Russians and Americans all complain that their contributions to world culture are neglected in the textbooks of other nations. If the English minimize the rôle of other peoples, it is equally true that in French books European culture often appears as hardly more than a variation on Versailles. German books are proud of spreading *Kultur* by displacing Slavs with Germans, yet full of self-pity when it comes to describing the displacement of Germans with Slavs, in the interest of Slavonic culture. As for countries like Poland or Sweden or Holland or Spain, which once were strong and now are weak, they feel that their contributions to European culture in their heyday remain almost untaught in countries which have not yet suffered the same misfortune.

In other words, the basic problem of bias in history books is how to think ourselves out of the milieu in which we have been reared, to force ourselves into points of view which are strange to ourselves but familiar elsewhere. Once again, we ought to heed Matthew Arnold's plea to learn and to propagate the best that is known and thought in the world: Goldsmith's letters from a Citizen of the World warning his western contemporaries against neglecting the cultural values of the East: and Toynbee's insistence in our time that 'the mental— or rather spiritual—feat that is required of us is to burst the cramping bounds of our English or French or German or American prison-house, whichever of the nationalities it may be that has been holding us hidebound'.

'Hidebound': that is the crucial word. Hidebound by the cultural traditions which we inherit, and by the traditions of learning which we acquire in our educational environment, we have learnt a hidebound history from teachers who were hidebound without knowing it, and without knowing it we teach a hidebound history to our pupils, who will grow up hardly less hidebound than ourselves. Our mouths are full of clichés which we have never challenged for ourselves. We speak of 'oriental duplicity', as though business methods were unknown in the West; of 'Prussianism', as though militarism were absent from the armies of other lands; of 'tyranny', as

though it were wrong to rule rigorously; of 'oligarchy', as
though the many were more enlightened than the few; of
'perfide Albion', as though treachery were a British monopoly; of '*Kultur*', as though non-Germans were necessarily
barbarians; of 'scratching a Russian and finding a Tartar',
as though the arts from Gogol to Diaghileff counted for
nothing.

The very vocabularies of our textbooks abound in this
unconscious prejudice. There can be a world of contempt in
the way we use adjectives like native, coloured, black, Negro.
In Britain, the word 'democracy' carries (in spite of Plato)
strong implications of excellence; in some other places it
implies inefficiency; and in Communist countries, though its
meaning is a good one, it is not at all the same as ours.
When we say '*Junker*' do we (like the Germans whose
language it is) mean a 'squire', or a militant and tyrannical
landlord? Why does 'Hellenic' mean something superior in
art, and 'Hellenistic' something inferior—like 'Gothic' in the
eighteenth century?

Besides this misunderstanding of specific words, there is
the bias which we introduce into our history books by verbal
nuances that are barely noticeable. Textbook writers rarely
notice that they are taking sides when they speak of the
'murder' of Nicholas II or Edward II, but of the 'execution'
(with all its implication of legal sanction) of Charles I or
Louis XVI. We are hardly being impartial when we call the
splitting of the Catholic Church a 'Reformation', or when
we describe as 'martyrdom' the fate of Hus on one side or
Joan of Arc on the other. To call the most famous of ancient
wars 'Peloponnesian' means that we are half consciously
aligning ourselves with the Athenians—from whom, in fact,
we have learnt almost all we know about it. Hannibal and
Scipio fought one another, we say, not in a 'Roman' but in a
'Punic' war, because we depend mostly on Roman sources

and look at the whole thing from the Roman point of view. The damage done by such partisanship among dead and gone antagonisms is not necessarily so irrelevant to our modern interests as it may seem at first. Schoolboys take sides with the Athenians against the Spartans and with the Romans against the Carthaginians; and having taken sides at school, they grow up into adults with a real though hazy conviction that European culture has done better by taking its cue from Athens instead of Sparta, and by being 'Romanized' instead of being 'Punicized'—though Nietzsche and the Nazis had their doubts about the first, and more learned men still have their doubts about the second.

All these are examples of the bias of inertia. We are so accustomed to thinking along well-worn lines that we rarely make the intellectual effort needed to strike out along lines of our own. Generations of teachers teach what they learned when they were young; generations of scholars learn what they will teach to others: and therefore the history taught in schools and universities lags far behind the new world for which it is supposed to prepare its citizens. The education of our times is at a cross-roads more critical even than education at the time of the Renaissance; if there was need, in the sixteenth century, for new school subjects and new kinds of textbooks, the need is vastly greater in the twentieth. No doubt the change should come slowly, for in education rapid change usually entails great dangers. But the change had better come, and of all the non-scientific subjects it is history which faces the greatest challenge. History teachers need to seek a fresh point of view and a fresh vocabulary to express fresh ideas. And they need to teach aspects of history which have hitherto been neg-lected, from minor matters of the European archives to the vast expanses of whole histories of the East. We need to teach far more than we do about our European neighbours: about the real history of the East our teaching has not yet

begun, and it will be generations before we can persuade ourselves to give the East its historical due.

*   *   *

Is this all practicable? How is the time to be found for
expansion of interest and subject-matter in history-lessons
and time-tables already crowded to bursting point? All over
Europe the usual allowance for teaching history to pupils in
their early teens is two or three periods a week, and in every
country teachers complain that they cannot fit everything
in. What is the use of suggesting the inclusion of yet more
material?

Merely to ask these questions is to betray misunderstanding
of the whole issue. We are dealing, not with mathematical
quantities of time or anything else, but with human minds
and societies. If it is true that there is no time at present to
teach world history, it is still more true that not to teach it is
becoming fatal. So long as every people remains ignorant of
the basic ideals and cultures of other peoples, disaster will
always be, as now, just round the corner. In a world which
can be circumnavigated in a week it is quite as important for
British children to learn the history of Europe as the history
of Britain, and quite as important to learn the history of Asia
as the history of Europe. It is not as though we were making
the best use of our time at present. Can anyone pretend that
we have no time for Akhnaton or Buddha or Asoka or Al
Hazen while we are finding time for Caractacus and Gaveston
and Lambert Simnel and Titus Oates and dozens of others as
insignificant? No time for the civilizations of Hans and Sungs
and Mongols and Moghuls and Arabs while we make time for
brasses and seals and four-centred arches and stocking-frames
and Crompton's mule and Stephenson's Rocket? No time for
the law-codes of Hammurabi or Justinian or Napoleon instead
of frankpledge or mortmain or copyholders and what not in

1832? Or to take one single century—the sixteenth. Need English children learn little or nothing about the arts of the Renaissance or the beginnings of capitalism or the achievements of Turkey and Poland and Russia and Aztecs and Akbar and the Tokugawa Shogunate and the new Astronomy of Tycho Brahe and Kepler and Galileo, while they are being stuffed with details about Empson and Dudley and the wives of Henry VIII and the Field of the Cloth of Gold and annates and religious atrocities and political massacres? The rejection of trifles would make room for a good deal of vital significance in world history which at present is ignored.

In any case, we need only to continue a process which has already begun. The history of one generation is always proving unsatisfactory to the next, and we could well treat our present dead growth much as our predecessors treated Alfred and the cakes or the fantastic misrepresentation of the tactics of Bannockburn which passed muster for history at the beginning of this century.

Still, it will not be enough to discard merely the unnecessary or the wrong. There is so much for which we ought to find room that we shall have to get rid of a good deal which is undoubtedly valuable—merely because to retain it will involve excluding things more valuable still. Our choice is not between the useless and the useful, but between valuable subjects among which priorities must be assessed. Rejecting the non-essential is comparatively easy; what has to be tackled is the far harder task of rejecting what we have always taught, and have always thought it important to teach. We need a revolutionary 'self-denying ordinance', followed by a 'new model' which will cause offence to all but the least conservative. What we have to do, in fact, is to re-assess our basic values. History is a medium of education, and we are educating not a leisured class like that for which Arnold started the teaching of history (and shocked the conservatives by doing so), but people who will have to face problems, political and social, of which Arnold could never have dreamed. The history which could equip Tom Brown for adult life will not do for the kind of adults into whom our pupils will grow. Hardly any of them need to learn the traditions and duties of an upper class. All of them are going to live in a world where the working classes have powers and obligations inconceivable to the employees of Tom Brown and his contemporaries: a world in which even England counts for less than it did, and the United States, Russia, India and China for far more. The political environment today is world-wide, and very little of the world is democratic in any English sense. Teaching the history of democracy is less necessary than it was a hundred years, or even fifty years, ago. Even democracy in the modern world is mostly unparliamentary, and therefore it is less important than formerly to learn the antecedents of parliament.

In fact, there is less need to know how and why parliamentary democracy has succeeded in England than how and why it has failed nearly everywhere else. The world is still ruled by dictators more than by democrats; the dictators are more powerful than they have ever been, and they seem to be on the increase. English education ought to show how dictatorships have succeeded or failed; the statesmanship of Pericles or Elizabeth I or Frederick the Great is more relevant to the world we live in than that of the Gracchi or Walpole or even Gladstone.

Dare we face the inexorable consequence? The dilemma has only two horns. If we are to find room for the most essential, we must reject the less essential. If we ought to include more about dictatorship, we shall have to exclude some of what we have been saying about parliament. If it is true that our time is insufficient, we shall have to jettison things which we do not want to jettison, in order to include what it has become vital to include. We could, for example, resolutely if reluctantly throw out of our history lessons all mention of such comparative side-issues as the Witan, the Mad Parliament, the Star Chamber, even the rotten boroughs and the Chartists. Reluctantly indeed, but resolutely, if we are sincere in our complaints that time is lacking for matters yet more vital than these in the education of the modern citizen of the world. Dare one even whisper the wisdom of deferring to the very latest teens all mention of such things as Magna Carta (that constitutional bubble blown in the early seventeenth century and burst in the early twentieth), or the Model Parliament (which after all proved unique), or the Petition of Right (which perhaps was never law, and in any case had to be re-enacted at the Revolution), or the legalistic details of the nineteenth-century parliamentary reforms, all of which were too soon superseded to be worth memorizing? All this might of course mean that many English children would leave school without ever being taught anything about Magna Carta; but it might also mean that time could be found to tell them something about the contemporary achievements of Genghis Khan, which have proved far more momentous for mankind than everything which happened in England during that most momentous century of English history. King John was not a world-figure: Genghis Khan was. Magna Carta was not a world-shaking event: the Mongol Empire was. If we must choose between them, which shall we teach our children about?

A very little reflection will reveal similar anomalies in any century of recorded history. To take only a few random examples of the way in which our textbooks devote more space to the less important, and less space to the more important, of conspicuous contemporaries. They say far more about Nebuchadnezzar than about Thales, far more about Pericles than about Socrates, far more about Hannibal than about Archimedes, about Bede than all the T'angs, about Ethelred than Avicenna, about Charles the Bold than all the artists of the Renaissance, Sacheverell than Tull, Peel than Liebig and Lawes combined, Disraeli than Darwin, Hitler than Einstein and the nuclear physicists put together. We in the West are too conscious of the power of politics, too indifferent to the power of things non-political that have influenced the lives of generations far more than politics have ever done.

It is the same with movements as with persons. We tend to dwell on many matters which have after all proved un-influential, and to say much less about matters which have turned the world upside down. A book which spares lengthy chapters for the constitution of Sparta or the frontier defences of the Roman Empire or the Wars of the Roses or the architectural vanities of Louis XIV can omit altogether such vital movements as the world-wide religious surge of the sixth and fifth centuries B.C., or the cultural and racial turmoil in the lands between India and the Mediterranean at the time of the Roman Empire, or the early emergence of Russia, or the entire civilization of the Far East, all of which have stamped their characters very deeply indeed upon the world of today. While this sort of thing remains true, it is idle for history teachers to pretend that their lessons and their text-books are too full to take in more. There will be space enough for the weightier matters we neglect at present when we have thrown overboard some of that super-cargo with which we still permit ourselves to be encumbered.

3

Clio Abused

WHEN a modern Englishman talks about falsifying history, he is usually thinking about Germans or Russians. Somewhere between 1900 and 1914 Germany ceased to be the home of scientific objectivity and became the home of lies. Soon after 1944 Russia ceased to be a source of literary and artistic truth and became the home of false doctrines. In both cases there is a good deal to be said for the changed attitude; but in both cases it was obviously too sudden and too superficial, and there is urgent need for a drastic re-appraisal of western views about German and Russian thought in general, not least German and Russian thought about history and its teaching.

Contrary to common belief, when writing history it is hard, not easy, to tell the truth. But the Nazis, as we all know, used their history, deliberately and coolly, for the fostering of falsehood. We all know this because we have been told it so often. But how many of us know what we really mean by it? How many of us have ever read a Nazi history book? It is well worth while, in order to see what exactly it is that the Nazis did to their history and how they did it.

The task is easy enough. There is no need to search among the vast spate of published nonsense which appeared under the Nazi régime. In this, the Nazis were not much better or worse than politicians in many other countries. All countries have their cranks in abundance, who publish nonsense which can be quoted by their adversaries in peace or war to show that their peoples are fools or knaves or both. It is not cranks with whom we are concerned, but the mass of normal Nazi opinion about history. The best place to find that is not in philosophical or even academic writings, however brilliant or foolish, but in the school textbooks. It is the business of a textbook to be commonplace: the school history books of any country contain the commonplaces of its historical thinking. If we want to know what historical orthodoxy under the Nazi régime was, we shall find it in the Nazi textbooks.

Fortunately for our purpose, there is only one book which we need examine. Unlike any English government, but like most other governments elsewhere, the Nazis exercised a rigorous control over their school books. In most highly-civilized countries the authors put into history textbooks not what they like, but what the government wishes; and the books which get closest to what the government wishes are the ones which the government imposes on the schools. If we blame the Nazis for doing this, we must also blame the governments of nearly every other country, including countries which are undoubtedly democratic, and a number of which are British.

In most places the practice is to provide a list of books from which the teachers may choose; the length of the lists varies enormously, from hundreds to just two or three. A few countries (including at least one West European democracy) have reduced their list to a single book, which is compulsory in all schools. After a long period of trial and error, this is what the Nazis at last did in 1944. By then, it was Nazi policy to have all school books published by a government department, and in history this policy was actually carried out. From 1944 there was only one history text for secondary schools: it was in three short books, and was called *Der Weg zum Reich—The Road to the Reich*. In that book we can find all we need for an understanding of the Nazi attitude to history and its teaching.

The first thing to look for is deliberate lies—statements contrary to the facts as known to competent historians. Of these, we shall find none whatever. The Nazis were far too clever propagandists for that. Lies are bad propaganda— sooner or later they reveal themselves. Hitler, it is true, declared that the bigger the lie, and the more often it is told, the more likely it is to be believed. Nevertheless, the conception of a vast German propaganda machine grinding out a grist of lies for sprinkling among all printed matter is one of the major phantasies of wartime. In school books, particularly, it would always be difficult and even useless to insist on the insertion of what is known to be untrue. School books are written and used by teachers accustomed by training and habit to sift evidence and opinion; to such men (of whatever nationality) writing or teaching lies would go heavily against the grain. Besides, the books are read by young people who delight in discovering and exposing the mistakes of their elders. No government, however efficient its ministry of propaganda, could get away with a policy of mass-lying in the schools. Consequently, it is difficult to find in the Nazi books any passages which can be quoted for their evident falsity. Any single sentence taken from *Der Weg zum Reich* is pretty certain to be true, or at any rate reasonable. *Der Weg zum Reich* is not a pack of lies; yet it would not be unjust to say that it is false from cover to cover.

Its principal fault, apparent on every page, is that it seeks to teach not the objective truth, but the policy of a party. No doubt the out-and-out Nazi teacher believed party policy and the truth to be synonymous. But only a minority of German teachers were ever out-and-out Nazis— or out-and-out anything, though a few of them, even in Nazi times, were out-and-out democrats. But Nazi or non-Nazi, all German

teachers had to use the Nazi history book; and the Nazi
history book was untrue—not untrue to facts, but stupen-
dously untrue to history. The facts are reasonably accurate:
the impression left on the pupils' minds is wrong.

Take, for instance, that stale bone of contention the battle
of Waterloo. Here is the account given by *Der Weg zum
Reich*:

> 'Napoleon had thrown himself immediately on the
> English commander-in-chief Wellington at Waterloo, in
> the hope of a speedy decision. Wellington, however, trust-
> ing in the promise of Prussian assistance, stood his ground.
> By forced marches the Prussians succeeded in reaching the
> battlefield, and attacked the French on the flank. Their
> arrival decided the issue. Napoleon was defeated, followed
> immediately by Gneisenau, and his army completely
> liquidated.'

Not a single statement there can be challenged as untrue,
yet the general impression conveyed is the very opposite of
the usual English version, which gives credit for the victory
to Wellington, and to the Germans merely the mopping up
of a retreating army. Perhaps Wellington's own verdict hit
the truth—'It was a damned near thing.' No doubt both the
German and the English versions are unfair to English and
Germans respectively.

In fact, *Der Weg zum Reich* resembles all other history
books in fostering misconceptions, not by inaccuracy of statement, but by selection among statements which are accurate.
We are not unfamiliar with this in Britain, where our history has
been dominated for over a century by a Whig interpretation.
The difficulty with all these interpretations of history—Whig,
Nazi or whatever—is that given their own hypotheses they
are accurate, and it is therefore difficult to pin-point their
errors. Their inaccuracy consists in faulty hypotheses, and in

vague nuances of phrasing which support those hypotheses. For instance, there is the favourite German doctrine of encirclement: *Der Weg zum Reich* makes great play of this throughout, but nowhere is it suggested that the disadvantages of 'encirclement' are offset by the advantages of a central striking-position. In the twentieth century Germany is encircled by French, Russians and British; in the sixteenth century Charles V is encircled by French and Turks; seven hundred years earlier Charlemagne himself is encircled by Saxons and Slavs and Moors.[1] But what does it all mean? If it means that Germans are surrounded by foreigners on most of their frontiers, then it is no more or less true of Germany than of any other land without an extensive seaboard. If, however, it implies a deliberate convergence of foes upon a central victim, then it ought not to be applied to Charlemagne, or Charles V, or Hitler.

'Encirclement' is only one of a number of words twisted to Nazi purposes in this Nazi school-book. Versailles is of course represented as a 'dictated' peace, forced by deceiving foes upon a deluded Germany; but the idea is pushed back into earlier history, so that we read, for example, of the *'Tilsiter Diktat'*. Throughout history, in fact, Germany's foes are made to act from villainous and the Germans themselves from innocent motives. Louis XIV's wars against the Dutch are 'plunder-wars', in the course of which 'German lands are raped'—and there are fuller details about the French devastation of the Rhineland in 1689 than about any German devastation of any country in any war. In 1914 'England willed the war', in order to buttress her world-wide empire, after having 'set Japan on Russia' in 1904, and 'annexed Tibet, thus shutting Russia away from India'. The picture painted of

[1]There is a picture-map to illustrate Charlemagne's conquest of these enemies, and their acknowledgment of his mastery. But whereas the Bohemian is German enough to be represented as merely bowing before the Kaiser, the Slav is drawn grovelling on the ground.

the British Empire, is, in fact, so different from any British conception that it is worth a quotation at some length:

'The English World-Empire spanned the whole earth. After the War of American Independence they had little more than Canada. Then they settled themselves firmly in Africa, and established British South Africa. Next they entered India and Australia, so that the Indian Ocean became a British sea. Soon the English policy fastened on East Asia, and established there strong points such as Singapore, Hong-Kong, Borneo and New Guinea. Strong-points the world over were the pillars of this world-Empire. Above all, the English were determined to make sure of their Indian colony. So they lined the sea-route from the Mother country with impregnable outposts like Gibraltar, Cyprus, Alexandria and Aden. To make sure of the land-route they sought to control Palestine and Iraq. An enormous navy gave this empire still greater security. With their world-supremacy the 40,000,000 English had a living-space three times as big as Europe and with more than 400,000,000 inhabitants. Still more important were the immense supplies of raw materials which they commanded. England, with her Jew-controlled commerce, fixed the price of tea, rice, timber and rubber. All the world was dominated by this Anglo-Jewish trading spirit'.

In contrast to the British Empire, the building of the German Reich appears almost a religious crusade, with the Third Reich of Adolf Hitler as the inevitable culmination of German history. The whole book is divided into three parts, each with the Reich as its main theme—the medieval Reich, or Holy Roman Reich of the German Nation; the Prussian fight for the Lesser German Reich; and the Greater German Reich of Adolf Hitler; and the theme is reinforced by three maps on the cover of the book. Within each of the parts the

Reich is the dominant *motif*, picked out by paragraph headings: 'The Reich begins' in the days of Clovis; Karl der Grosse 'expands and strengthens it'; Henry the Fowler 'establishes a Volksreich'; Kaiser Otto I 'confirms the unity of the Reich' and 'secures its eastern frontier'; Barbarossa makes '*Reich und Kaisertum*' illustrious; Henry the Lion 'strengthens the Reich in the East'; German peasants in the Middle Ages 'stand up for the Reich and for Europe'; in the days of the Hapsburgs 'the strength of the Reich declined'; the Renaissance and Reformation 'shook' it; 'the Treaty of Westphalia cut the Reich to pieces'; 'Prussia became the Leader of the Reich'; at the time of Napoleon, 'the Reich ceases to exist'; during the nineteenth century, 'Austria hindered its Unity'; while 'Prussia strove to mould the Imperial Unity'; 'Bismarck was the architect of the Lesser German Reich'. The remaining two-fifths of the whole history course is devoted mainly to the rise of Adolf Hitler and 'his' Reich.

Not one of these headings is demonstrably untrue; but their cumulative effect is to produce an impression of German history which is quite unbalanced.

From time to time there emerges some '*Reichsfeind*'— Enemy of the Empire. In the early middle ages it is the Slavs; in modern times it is the French; and in all periods the Jews are '*Volksfeind*'—the Enemy of the People. Though confined to the ghetto, they 'spread abroad everywhere' making a profit of their trade, charging 'shameless interest . . . sometimes amounting to 174 per cent'. The French Revolution showed the danger of granting the Jews equal rights, which 'enabled them to exercise their corrupting influence on the French people'. In the nineteenth century 'the Jews began to work openly and energetically against the unity of the Reich'; 'their excessive riches enabled them to intermarry with the nobility', and 'they entered the Civil Service, the Press, and Politics,

and dominated Art'. Marx was 'the son of a Jewish Rabbi', and
in the late nineteenth and early twentieth centuries Jewry
became international and 'strove to dominate the world'. It did
what it could to 'further the war' against Germany; in the
nineteen-thirties it tried 'to seize Spain in order to complete
the encirclement of Germany from the west'; and in the
second world war 'the Jews worked on the receptive President
Roosevelt, as in the First World War they had upon the
internationalist Wilson', with the result that 'America supported the Anglo-Jewish drive against the Axis'.

Here, again, it is difficult to pick out any single statement
as indubitably false. Yet there is an obvious build-up of
falsity, and this rises to its climax in dealing with the history
of Nazism itself. In the first place, of this whole course cover-
ing German history from its beginnings to the twentieth
century, about a quarter is devoted to the work of Hitler and
the Nazi Party. The entire party programme is printed in full
in two pages of small type. Nearly a whole page gives in thick
type the names of the sixteen Nazis killed during the unsuccessful *putsch* in 1923: that is, more space is allotted to sixteen almost unknown victims of one day's abortive rising
than to the whole of the French Revolution or the events of
1848. The fourteen years of the Weimar régime get four pages,
the eleven years of Nazi power forty-seven. Hitler's life is told
in full; even Göring, though less prominent, is given far more
detail than, for instance, the Emperor Joseph II.

During the same period military history is kept well in the
limelight. This, no doubt, was partly due to the value placed
by Nazi philosophy on fighting and war. But it was also due
to the wisdom of the propaganda machine. Children like to
read about fighting, and this book makes the most of the
military appeal—and of other appeals to young readers.
Though published during the economic exigencies of war, its
appearance is more attractive than that of the textbooks of the

pre-Nazi period. The type is easy to read, and it is varied to suit the varying emphasis of the subject-matter. Headings are succinct, clear and easy to remember. There are plenty of illustrative diagrams and picture-maps, some of them tinted to emphasize the main theme. Above all, perhaps, it avoids the common fault of most previous German schoolbooks: it is not inordinately long. It is, in fact, pleasantly short. The whole of German history in 250 pages—two or three at most would suffice for a night's homework. There is none of that fantastic stuffing out of children's minds so characteristic of German textbooks in earlier (and, alas, in later) times. The Road to the Reich must have seemed a primrose path to harassed history teachers under the Nazis.

And if it was in fact a primrose path of propaganda, we need to remember that it would not seem so to the majority of German teachers. Shocking as much of it must appear to others, Germans would find most of it quite familiar. There were no new notes in the historical paean of the Nazis—only old notes struck much more loudly, and in unison, with the counterpoint left out. Most of the Nazi teaching about history is not Nazi at all. It is German—and it can be found in German history books published long before Nazism was born. Against the stirdency of the Nazi textbook those of the Weimar period may sound innocuous; they were, in fact, re-imposed on the schools by the victorious Allies in 1945. Yet Stresemann was as good a German as Hitler. Becker, the Prussian minister of education from 1925 to 1930, was probably more patriotic than the education minister of the Nazis. But it was Becker who issued the famous directive of 1925 telling German history teachers to emphasize such topics as encirclement, the superiority of the German race, its claims to dominate Europe, and the principle of Leadership (*Führertum*) beloved of Germans long before the days of Hitler. If *Der Weg zum Reich* maintained that in 1939 England willed the war, the textbooks of the Weimar Republic taught that in 1914 'there was no wish for war in Berlin', and that 'today every informed person inside and outside Germany knows that Germany is absolutely innocent with regard to the outbreak of war, and that Russia, France and England wanted the war and unleashed it'. At the same period German books were insisting that Alsace was overwhelmingly German (as in population it was, though not in culture) and were leaving it to be assumed that Lorraine was the same. Another favourite theme was the German occupation of Poland. There was no proclamation here of the rights of race. Where there were Germans, the land should be German. But that criterion was not applied to other countries. In Poland the Poles had mismanaged their affairs: since the partition, German rule had changed Poland from a neglected wilderness to an agricultural and industrial paradise, and that justified the German occupation. As for the Hague conference of 1899, it was not Kaiser William who frustrated the disarmament proposals there; they were cold-shouldered by all the powers, and Germany alone was honest enough to say so. In all these things the Weimar books were not only forecasting ideas of the Third Reich, they were echoing ideas of the Second, when books were as fulsome about the Kaiser as they were later to be about Hitler—or as British books had already been about Queen Victoria.

*   *   *

After the Nazi collapse and the great burning of the books in 1945 the new rulers of eastern Germany, like their allies in the West, had to cast about for emergency history books to fill the gap until they could produce satisfactory books of their own. The western Allies, as we have seen, fell back upon textbooks of the Weimar period, with their shaky parliamentary democracy. Similarly, the Russians in eastern Germany found their stop-gap among socialist books written before Nazi times. The most useful, in fact, had been written even before the First World War, in the palmy days of German socialism. In 1947 a new school edition was published of Mehring's *German History Since the End of the Middle Ages*, which was originally written in 1910. This was seven years too early for Bolsheviks brought up on the principles of 1917. But it was socialist enough to manage for the time being, and it was new-furnished with a biographical index and a glossary of technical terms (mostly political) which tilted it in the Bolshevik direction.

The original book had been something of a landmark. It embodied not only the rising reaction of those days against drum and trumpet history, but also that against what we in Britain came later to call the Whig interpretation: the writing of history as though its natural goal had been parliamentary democracy. Mehring insisted on treating the Reformation, for example, not as a step towards the freeing of parliaments from kings, but as a capitalistic and bourgeois interlude between a society which was feudal and a society which was socialist. The same view was taken of the English Revolution of the seventeenth and the French Revolution of the eighteenth centuries. All these were mere preliminaries to the real workers' revolutions of the nineteenth and twentieth centuries, and the establishment of the socialized society. The Peasants' Revolt was more important than Luther, and Louis Blanc was more important than Louis Napoleon. Moreover, social history, and the history of thought in literature, were given a prominence not at all usual in history books in 1910. There were lengthy appreciations of Lessing, Goethe, Kant, among others. On the whole, these appreciations were fair and objective; there was very little in them of which any western parliamentarian would be likely to complain.

But when the book was reissued as an educational instrument thirty years after the Russian Revolution, it needed some bringing into line; and this was done in new appendices, written not by Mehring himself, but by the desperately hurried anti-Nazis of 1945. Consequently, the appendices are blatantly propagandist. Lessing and Kant become 'bourgeois'. Goethe, the protégé of a duke, 'opposed the French Revolution' because 'he had little understanding of the bourgeois epoch which was just beginning'. Heine was 'influenced by the friendship of Marx'. Hegel's chief importance was as 'the discoverer of the laws of dialectic, and the first to make conscious use of them'. In the glossary, democracy is, 'literally, "supremacy of the people": but in capitalistic states, a supremacy of the capitalists under parliamentary forms. A true democracy is possible only when the working classes are in possession of political power'.

All this, for a school book, seems tendentious enough. But it is nothing compared with the treatment of great names in British history. Here are three entries from the biographical summary, each given in full:

DARWIN, C. R. (1809–1882): One of the greatest English naturalists. Founder of the theory of evolution. 'Darwin's writings are the scientific basis for the historic idea of class warfare' (Marx).

That, perhaps, is fair. Evolution is a political as well as a biological conception, and certainly Darwin's work contributed to political evolutionism. But did it contribute to nothing else, as this entry implies?

Here is the second entry:

MILTON, John (1608–1674): Poet of the English Revolution.

That is all. Nothing about the greatest religious epic in English literature; nothing about Puritanism, or even about the early lyrics. Milton's rôle in history is reduced to pure politics. Finally, with Shakespeare the book topples head over heels into propagandist absurdity:

SHAKESPEARE, William (1564–1616): English poet, one of the most important dramatists in world literature. Wrote his works in the epoch of rising manufacture, of the transition from feudalism to bourgeoisie, and the beginnings of English commercial supremacy. Very highly esteemed by Marx and Engels.

It would be difficult to find any better example of the kind of history which is every bit true and yet altogether false.

*   *   *

We need, however, to be constantly reminding ourselves that 'truth' and 'falsehood' mean different things to different people. Nazi, Fascist, Communist propagandists believe themselves to be propagating not what is false but what is true. Consequently, it is useless to confront them with their own propaganda and expect them to be ashamed of it. They see no reason for shame, or even for concealment. The Russians have gone out of their way to translate and publish in western Europe particulars about their own use of history in schools. English translations are available both of the standard history textbook for Russian secondary schools and of official instructions of various kinds. Between them we can get a good idea of what the Russian government wants from its history teachers.

First, the textbook itself[1]. It is issued in three volumes, illustrated, though for some reason there are no maps. The first volume stops about 1640, for to Communists the English

[1] *A History of the U.S.S.R.*, edited by A. M. Pankratova: Foreign Language Publishing House, Moscow, 1948.

Civil War is an event of world significance; it marks the end of the 'feudal' period of history. Volume II carries the story to about 1900. This leaves the stage clear for the advent of Leninism during the twentieth century.

As an instrument for teachers the whole book must be very inefficient. Its format is unattractive, it is too long for school children, its language and thought are often well above the capacity of normal adolescents. There are strings of unrelated facts. Legend is often accepted uncritically as history. Wilful exaggerations and distortions are everywhere. It is, in fact, about the level of our own history books in late Victorian times.

Communists claim that the books are 'objective' and 'factual'. To non-Communists they will seem anything but that. To begin with, the whole attitude of the five authors is propagandist. Children's feelings are played upon in a way regarded by us as unworthy. 'Heroic Russian soldiers' are eternally beating cowardly foreign soldiers; or, if they themselves happen to be beaten, it is the fault of the generals, who are members of the 'exploiting classes'—until 1917; after that, Russian armies may be outnumbered, but neither soldiers nor generals do anything wrong.

This artificial stimulation of patriotism appears in many other ways. In war after war Russia is represented as saving civilization from disaster. She it was who 'took the brunt of the Tartar invasion'. 'In August 1805 the entry of the Russian troops into Europe frustrated Napoleon's plans for a forced crossing of the Channel and saved England from invasion.' Napoleon was not beaten by the winter in 1812: 'the weather was mild. . . . It was the spirit of the Russian nation, the magnificent heroism and staunchness of the Russian army, supported by the whole nation, which encompassed Napoleon's defeat'. In 1914, 'by taking the blow upon herself Russia saved her ally France from defeat'. 'In 1941, the Soviet Union actually fought Germany single-handed.' 'Churchill, bent on satisfying the mercenary interests of British imperialism, resorted to all sorts of devices to hold up the opening of the Second Front, and to inflict as much damage as possible on our state. . . . The Soviet army's victories were a decisive factor in ensuring the Allies military successes in North Africa and Italy.'

Every country exaggerates its own contribution to civilization, but these books sometimes seem almost to claim civilization as a Russian monopoly. One cannot complain of the insistence that lessons should teach the pupil 'patriotic pride in their country, and in the glorious past of the Russian people', or even in 'the priority of Russian scholars, inventors and travellers'. There is, in fact, more than a hint of inferiority complex in the claim of the official syllabus of 1952 that 'demonstrating the priority of Russian culture in many fields is an important means of combating possible instances of cringing before things foreign'. But the process is carried too far. Russian scientists apparently unknown to English histories of science are represented as pioneers in all kinds of progress. Lomonosov was 'the first to demonstrate the vegetable origin of coal', and to formulate the law of conservation of mass, later 'rediscovered by Lavoisier'; 'he was almost sixty years ahead of Young in establishing the type of undulatory vibrations of the earth's surface'; 'thirty years ahead of Herschel in discovering the presence of an atmosphere on Venus': '135 years ahead of Nansen in indicating the direction of drift in the Arctic Ocean'. Polzunov invented the steam engine and was 'twenty-one years ahead of Watt' in adapting it for use in factories. Petrov 'discovered electrolysis independently of Nicholson and Carlisle', and 'created the Voltaic arc several years before Davy'. 'Schilling constructed the first electromagnetic telegraph in the world at Petersburg in 1832.' Jakobi built the first electric boat. Mendeleyev

C

'discovered the periodic law and created the periodic system of elements', and here politics is permitted to intrude into science, for 'Marx and Engels placed great value on Mendeleyev's discovery, which they regarded as a triumph of dialectic materialism'. 'Popov was the celebrated inventor of wireless telegraphy (1895)'; 'Yablochkov invented the first electric arc lamp in the world'; 'Ladygin created the first incandescent electric lamp'. Russia was 'the birthplace of the science of aviation'; the first aeroplane was constructed by Mozhaiski in the 1880's. Tsiolkovski built a dirigible balloon ten years before the first Zeppelin, and he also 'formulated the principles of the jet-propelled engine'. Finally, for what it is worth, not Florence Nightingale but 'Dasha Sevastopolskaya was the first nurse in the world to tend the wounded at the war'. Of course, any or all of these claims may be well-founded; some of them certainly are. Experts must decide between the very different accounts current in Russia and in the West. But surely there are too many of them to carry conviction, unless sputniks have made the West easier to convince of the claims of Russian science.

All this is propaganda (justified or not) by asseveration. It is supplemented throughout by the more insidious forms of propaganda: omission and distortion. Tendentious epithets are everywhere, repeated far too often, one would think, even for the teaching of children. 'Toiling workers', 'exploited masses', 'slave-owning classes', 'predatory imperialists'— these and a host of others recur repeatedly throughout ancient, medieval and modern history. Subtle nuances of phraseology sow their seed of misunderstanding. During the partition of Poland, for example, 'Austria wished to *conquer*, Prussia to *annex* . . . Russia strove to *recover*' the Polish territories. No opportunity is lost of driving home desirable propaganda in politics. Trotsky and the Trotskyites are 'bandits' and 'bourgeois'; 'traitors' and 'chauvinists'. Stalin is always

'Comrade', and he is ranked in the hierarchy with Marx, Engels and Lenin—for the books were published in 1948. While Stalin is in the ascendant he 'must be the theme of a separate lesson', even though 'the biography of Lenin is not given as a separate topic'. The notorious 'cult of the individual' was extended backwards into the past: much was made of the medieval princes, of Ivan IV and Peter the Great and Catherine the Great. All of them had to be debunked in 1956 along with Stalin when teachers were told after all to discount their personal achievements.

During this anti-Stalin reaction of 1956 academic history suffered along with the history of the schools. *Voprosy Istorii*, a distinguished historical review, came under heavy fire. It had, they said, been too favourable to the Mensheviks in dealing with Russian history from 1905 to 1917. It had published too little about colonial imperialism, and in particular about American anti-Russian activity in 1917–18. It had neglected the origins of the Second World War, and the history of working-class movements outside Russia. It had relaxed its former ideological drive against American capitalism. It had been guilty of 'violation of party principles in the treatment of C.P.S.U. history'. It had failed, in fact, to realize that 'workers on the ideological front include historians', and that 'in assessing historical problems . . . this is the main point—a party-minded, Leninist approach to facts and developments'. It had 'thus to some extent damaged the ideological and political education of cadres'. Finally, 'the former Deputy-Editor in Chief often abandoned the principles of collective leadership, and acted on his own'. The Editorial Board was therefore changed, and in future the new Board 'will pay special attention to determined re-establishment of party principles in assessing historical phenomena'.

When history itself is thus subordinated to party manœuvres there can be no surprise that history teaching in schools and universities is bound hand and foot to the party line. 'The most important task of the school is the education of the children in Soviet patriotism, Soviet national pride'. That, perhaps, is not so bad. No worse, at any rate, than what used to be fashionable in Britain and is still fashionable all over western Europe and America. But directives do not stop at patriotism, or even national pride. One official syllabus insists that 'cultural matters must be approached primarily and fundamentally from the class point of view. . . . As a result of the course the pupils should understand that Soviet democracy is the only genuine democracy. . . . School courses of Social History must be based on the ideas contained in Marxist-Leninist classics'. An inspector complains that in one school a teacher 'has not understood his main task, which consists in carrying out the well-known instructions of Comrades J. V. Stalin, A. A. Zhdanov and S. M. Kirov, that the idea of contrast between bourgeois and social revolutions should form the very core of the entire course of Modern History'. In the same school unsatisfactory History is 'due to the low ideological standard of teaching. . . . Unfortunately there are still quite a number of teachers who have not learnt to subordinate their work to the most important tasks of ideological-political education'. It is the same with all periods. 'At the centre of the pupils' attention in the course of the history of the Ancient World there stands the question of slavery, the first form of exploitation of man by man, the first form of the division of society into classes. . . . The most important material of the course in the Middle Ages is the history of the class-struggle of the exploited classes against the exploiters. . . . The Modern History course is of very great importance in the formation of a Communist world-outlook among the pupils. . . . The radical difference between the great October Social Revolution and all bourgeois revolutions is the central question in the Modern History Course.'

'Ideological-political education' includes the teaching of an attitude towards religion, which comes in for its full share of antagonistic propaganda. It is not that the schools of Russia teach that this or that religion is wrong. But in the chapters on Religious History religion itself is rarely if ever mentioned. The teachings of Christianity are not contradicted; they are simply omitted as irrelevant. Calvinism is not Presbyterian, it is 'bourgeois' and 'capitalistic'. Luther was not the opponent of Catholic doctrines, he was the tool of the exploiting classes. The English Civil War is regarded as one of the turning-points of history, but there is no mention of any religious issue. According to one manual for history teachers, Christianity is merely one of the many religions with parallel doctrines and hagiology. Its chief value is as a weapon of political propaganda on behalf of the exploiting classes: 'the resort of a slave-class in a dissolving society'. ('In this connexion it is useful to narrate the myth of Jesus Christ' and 'the legend of the resurrection, because according to this myth nature responded with rejoicing to the fact of Christ's resurrection'.)[1] Another official directive insists that 'the teacher must constantly bear in mind the rôle of religion as a powerful weapon in the hands of the ruling classes. . . . The chief reason for the adoption of Christianity [in Russia in the early Middle Ages] was the fact that the class of feudal lords, which sprang up in the Dnieper region, needed a religion which would support its class interests'. One seeks in vain for any intimation that Christianity, or any of the religions of the Asian regions of Russia, had any ethical or spiritual content whatever.

[1] An official textbook of Ancient History for secondary schools apologizes for using the normal Christian system of dating: 'We adopt here the chronology which has long been recognized throughout the world, reckoning from the supposed birth of Jesus Christ. As a matter of fact, science has demonstrated that there never was a Jesus Christ. But until recently people believed in him, and regarded the year of his birth as the inauguration of an era, from which they counted their years.'

It needs perhaps to be repeated that in all this the Communists see nothing to be ashamed of. They say these things to one another, they include them in official reports and directives, they publish them, they even translate them (often very badly) for publication abroad. And in saying these things and in publishing them they think they are doing right, as we in the West do when we say and publish things about our own firm beliefs. There is, in fact, a complete cleavage between East and West in the reasons accepted for history teaching, and indeed for all education. We in the West regard truth as many-sided, and we encourage the expression of views from all sides. In the Communist view of history there is no place for such latitude. The truth about history has been stated for all time by Marx, and history must always be taught on Marxist principles. 'A teacher must understand that history is in itself, scientifically, i.e. in the light of the Marxist-Leninist outlook and truthful exposition [the two are evidently synonymous] a perfect weapon for the communist indoctrination of students. . . . History is a powerful weapon of communist education and must wholly serve the cause of the struggle for Communism.' And there must be no half-measures: 'the historical material must be so selected and expounded that it has an emotional effect upon the pupil . . . it must be indissolubly linked with the evocation in the children of hatred for the slavish past, for the exploiting classes, and the Tsarist order.'

From time to time there is a claim that the need to teach initiative on the part of the pupils is not overlooked. There must be 'ability to think historically and to understand a historical situation'. The *Times Educational Supplement*, reporting in 1952 on some Soviet textbooks, thought they discouraged 'simple black-and-white judgments', and that 'the child cannot help but learn that, for the greater part of human history, one cannot say "Yes" or "No" but must say

"Yes—but", or "No—but" '. Whether or no this is true of the textbooks, it can hardly stand up against the repeated insistence of official directives and manuals of pedagogy: 'a teacher must understand . . . the teacher must note. . . . He must show . . . teachers are first of all obliged to . . . the teacher must provide clear material on the revolts of the slaves and the poor . . . the teacher must bring the pupils to a realization of the following dictum of Comrade Stalin . . .'. How different from the same problem as seen by a French official directive: *'en dernière analyse, rien ne vaut que par le maître . . . son souci d'échapper à toute orientation, et toute propaganda'!*

The story is the same in other Communist countries. In Rumania, for instance, the textbooks divide all history into four significant periods—Primitive, Feudal (the Middle Age, which extends to 1750), Capitalist (1750–1917), and Socialist (since 1917). Russia, naturally enough, receives better treatment than any other foreign country. In the Peace Treaty of 1947, for example, all the clauses favourable to Rumania are attributed to Soviet diplomacy, all the unfavourable clauses are strongly resisted by the Russian delegates. The main aim of history teaching is 'to acquaint the student with the progressive forces of the past, with the struggle of the peasantry against feudal reaction, the . . . working classes against the forces of capitalism, and the . . . intellectuals against reactionary ideas'. Similarly, in Czechoslovakia one of the chief aims is 'to develop the sense of international solidarity of the workers', and the Czech books are full of the 'castes' and 'classes' and 'slavery' common to all Communist history.

Communist history, in fact, has a vocabulary of its own, with the same loaded epithets constantly repeated. At all periods of history there has been 'mass expropriation' by 'slave-owning classes', in ancient times 'aristocratic' and in modern times 'bourgeois', but always contrasted with the 'toiling peasants'. 'Progressive' means 'Communist', 'reactionary' means 'capitalistic'. And 'reactionary' is applied repeatedly to the clerical and priestly classes of all countries in all ages. All wars before 1917 were 'robber-wars', though in many of them there was good fighting by 'heroic Russians'. 1914–1918 was 'predatory', and though 1941–5 was 'the Great Patriotic War', in it, as before and since, it is necessary to distinguish the predatory activity of 'Anglo-American Warmongers'.

About Communist China there is little information available, but the Common Programme of the People's Republic includes 'the strengthening of propagandist education for the broad masses', and 'the application of the scientifical-historical viewpoint to the study and interpretation of History, Economics, Culture and International Affairs'. What 'scientific-historical' means is made clear in a Russian publication of 1948, which advocates history teaching because 'by cultivating and developing in students "historicism", i.e. an historic attitude with regard to the phenomena of social life, we establish in their consciousness the bases of dialectic thinking'.

*   *   *

All this betrays a view of history teaching which most teachers in western Europe and America find revolting. Yet why we find it revolting is a perpetual puzzle to the Communists, who believe in Communism, and think their children ought to be taught it. Besides, they say that we do the same sort of thing ourselves. And if we examine ourselves as ruthlessly as we do them, we shall find that we are not altogether guiltless. It may be that Clio is more abused elsewhere, but in the western home of parliamentary democracy she does not escape scot-free.

And here it is necessary for a British book to repeat what British teachers of history are constantly repeating and foreigners find it very difficult to believe: that history teaching in Britain is entirely free from official direction, and almost entirely free from official pressure. We have no government directives about history teaching. Our Ministry of Education does, indeed, publish a pamphlet called *Teaching History*, which is crammed with sound and sensible advice. But though most of us will wish to follow the advice, nobody is bound to take it, and nobody will suffer in any way for disregarding it. So long as they are reasonably efficient, British teachers of history may teach what they like how they like—and the more originality they show the better the officials seem pleased. Our Ministry does not even follow the almost universal practice of issuing a list of textbooks for teachers to choose from. Some of our local education authorities do this, but even they are thinking, not about any kind of indoctrination, political or otherwise, but of accuracy and scholarship and sound pedagogy. In the teaching of history, as in many other things, it is probably still true that we are the freest country in the world.

In this respect, indeed, *Teaching History* is an advance on its predecessors. All previous pamphlets issued by the Ministry assumed that one function of the history lesson is to produce democrats. Even that has gone now. *Teaching History* contains hardly a hint of propaganda on behalf of any cause whatever; not even parliamentary democracy, or that favourite of former generations, the British Commonwealth; not even patriotism, or Christianity. Almost every other government does claim patriotism at least as one fundamental aim of the history lesson; even the western democracies; even the United States; and of course the Communist countries. In Syria a non-Communist government says that 'to develop nationalism and nourish patriotism is the real aim of history teaching'. We go to the other extreme in England, where a Historical Association pamphlet insists that for history as for other social studies 'it is important to choose countries with geographical features strongly differentiated from our own, which in obvious ways have influenced their historical and social development, and with governmental peculiarities which also contrast with ours, and so emphasize and rouse interest in our own methods'. No doubt practice in Britain lags well behind these principles, but the principles are there, and it is important to note that not only have we no compulsion to teach along an official line, but even the encouragement we receive is in the direction of impartiality.

It is sometimes said that nationalism in history teaching is greatest in countries where nationalism itself is a new thing, and least in old countries whose national status has long been safe. This notion receives support in the case of Syria just quoted, and other examples could easily be produced. But, as we have seen, nationalism is well to the fore in Russia, international in outlook though Communism undoubtedly is. And even in the United States (about which it is difficult to generalize because educational policy varies from state to state) teaching seems far from free, and teachers are encouraged to inculcate ideas which are by no means universally accepted. One bitter article—*Are American Teachers Free?* published in 1936—goes so far as to maintain that teaching in America is subject to intensive interference from all sorts of pressure-groups—anti-German, anti-British, Big Business, and so on. Still, whether or no it is true, this view is not typical. There are plenty of American manuals urging impartiality on the teachers. 'The first duty of a teacher,' says one of them, 'is not to any organization, national or international, but to his pupil. The main object of education is not to produce a loyal national citizen, a good American, an internationally minded man: it is to produce a complete and, as far as possible, a happy person, in harmony with his inner self and his fellow-beings.' Others insist that a principal object of history teaching is to encourage pupils 'to form independent judgments in sifting what they read or hear', and 'to distinguish between fact and opinion'. Yet this last book contains a chapter on 'Developing Desirable Attitudes', and that, however desirable the attitudes may be, opens the door to abuse. Who is to decide what attitudes are 'desirable'? Belief in parliamentary democracy? One publication of the State University of New York has no doubt about that: 'Every pupil should have a conviction of the value of democratic political processes . . . the young citizen should have a clear realization of what political democracy means in his own country. . . . He should be alert to the threats which always confront democratic processes, but determined to expand rather than to curtail these processes.' To supporters of parliamentary democracy that may seem entirely harmless; but it would take a good deal to persuade a Communist that it is not exactly parallel with his own propagation of the political principle that 'as a result of the course the pupils should understand that Soviet democracy is the only genuine democracy'.

Besides, it needs to be borne in mind that the gulf between history teaching in the Communist and the non-Communist countries is often more verbal than real. We do not hammer to death repetitive epithets in the way Communists do, but at least we now admit that ancient Athens was a 'slave-economy', with more than a doubt whether its eternally belauded constitution was 'democratic' at all. We do not splatter our pages with the French word 'bourgeois', but it was we who in the days of the first Toynbee invented the idea of the 'Industrial Revolution' as a counterblast to the political revolution which preceded it, and we have emphasised the existence of 'exploited' and 'exploiting' classes at least since the Conservative Disraeli introduced us to 'Two Nations' in Britain over a century ago.

There are in fact some ways in which the Russian and other Communist history books are decidedly superior to ours. Communism is an international belief, and Communist history teaching is more international in character than that of the non-Communist countries. Obsessed as the Communists are by economics, they are less obsessed than we by politics. Their books do not, like ours, stress politics at the expense of culture. Great poets often receive as much notice as great statesmen: art and science are not denied a place, or squeezed into an afterthought. Above all, they have a view of world history far less narrow than that almost invariably found in the books of western Europe and America. It embraces much more about what we call the East—though to Russia it is hardly eastern at all. Not only do they give due space, in a way unparalleled in the West, to near-eastern cultures—Slav and Byzantine. They also say far more about Islam, and India, and China. In Russia this is natural enough, since geographically Russia is more in Asia than in Europe. But this is true of the other Communist countries, too. There are, of course, in the history and society of both India and China elements congenial to Communism. There is more to it than that, though. Whereas in western books it seems usual to elbow out from the normal human survey three-quarters of the human race, in these Communist books it seems unnatural. In short, the Orient gets fuller justice from the Communist historians than from the rest of us.

But not full justice: full justice to the East has never been done, in any history textbook ever published in any part of Europe or America.

4

East is East and East is West

FULL justice to the East has never been done in any history textbook ever published in any part of Europe or America.

During the later 1950's UNESCO decided that there were three world problems of greater urgency than any others, and these three were made the subject of 'Major Projects'—the UNESCO equivalent of Five-Year or Ten-Year Plans. One was the need to extend primary education in Latin America, where much education is not so much primary as primitive. Another was the development of arid lands, which still spread barrenness over a quarter or more of the earth's surface. The third was the removal of misunderstanding between East and West. And in order that the West and the East shall understand one another better, UNESCO has suggested that while western countries shall concentrate first of all on making known and understood the cultural values of the East, the eastern countries shall first concentrate on making known and understood the cultural values of—the East!

This is not so topsy-turvy as it sounds. The object of UNESCO is to persuade the East and the West to get to know one another equally well. UNESCO realizes, as every sensible person in the world should realize, that at present thinking people in the East know and understand a good deal about the culture of the West, whereas thinking people in the West know and understand next to nothing about the cultures of the East. In Asia, there are millions of educated Asians who speak one or more of the European languages, and hundreds of thousands who know something of one or more of the chief western literatures. How many educated Europeans or Americans speak any Asian language, or have ever read any Asian classic, except, no doubt, an Anglicized love poem produced in the leisure hours of that eminent eastern mathematician Omar Khayyám? As for eastern culture in general, it is no exaggeration to say that we in the West know almost nothing about the fundamental values of the East. For one thing we never think or learn about the East except in a western connexion. When we speak of civilization, we mean the civilization of the Europeans; we give no thought to the civilizations of the East. We in England know and teach about Indian history little more than the activities of the English in India: about Clive and Warren Hastings and Bentinck and Dalhousie and Curzon; nothing about Asoka or Chandragupta or Mahomet of Ghazni or Akbar; about Plassey but not about Panipat; about Suttee but not about Bhakti. In Chinese history we know and teach only those episodes in which Englishmen were involved—the embassy of Macartney, the opium wars and the Treaty Ports and the Boxer Rebellion; nothing about Wu-Ti or Hsaio Wen or Tai Tsung or K'ang Hsi, or anything of which a Chinese could feel proud.

The same thing is true of every country in Europe and America. One of the activities set on foot by UNESCO's East-West Major Project has been the examination of western history textbooks, not by Orientals, but by western teachers themselves. From every country comes the same tale of misgiving. The best general statement of the position is, perhaps, that made by Belgian critics about Belgian books:

'Our view of the Middle Ages is systematically centred on Europe. A few brief allusions to Marco Polo and to adventurous voyages in Asiatic seas are all that we can rely upon to present to youthful minds the existence of a vast reservoir of human beings and unknown civilizations on the other side of the world. Our modern history is *our* modern history: Asia plays but a small rôle in it. Generally speaking, it is quite forgotten. If mention is sometimes made of south-east Asia, it is to speak of the Portuguese and Dutch establishments; if India is referred to, it is to honour the memory of Suffren or Dupleix. . . . The human side of history is left out of account. The school manuals tell us, perhaps, about the East India Company and the Indian Mutiny; but the Japanese, the Asiatic of whatever race, continues to remain a closed book. The ways of life, the social structures, the aspirations of these peoples remain veiled from us; we learn nothing of their standard of living, their level of education, the meaning of their religions, or their internal administration. The colonial and imperialist tradition is palpable in these pages; it is not as citizens of the world that we discover Asia.'

French critics of French books say much the same:

'There is a striking disproportion between the attention devoted to European expansion and colonization in Asia, on the one hand, and the great Asian civilizations on the other. . . . Events and civilizations outside Europe receive attention, and are attributed importance, in proportion to the connection (or at least the apparent connection) they have with the history of Western Europe. In the case of Asia, the further a region lies, geographically, from Western Europe, the fewer references are made to it.'

Swiss critics of Swiss books get down to statistics:

'This book is exclusively European in outlook. One and a half pages are allocated to Islam and the Arabs, two sentences to Mahomet. The author takes practically no account of the influence of the East on European civilization since the Crusades. Proportion, 2–3 per cent, for a book dealing exclusively with World History.'

The Italians found that:

'In several books, for instance, the history of India is confined to the history of British colonization. In some textbooks the history of China begins with the Treaty of Shimonoseki in 1895, as though the life of the Chinese people before that were of very little interest. . . . The children, either from that sort of mental indolence that leads to avoidance of new experiences, or from almost unconscious pride of race, are inclined to accept the statements commonly found in works of popular scholarship which credit the western races with the monopoly of culture, industry, scientific knowledge and progress.'

'Our history knows of Asiatic invasions . . . it knows of an Asian peril: but it says nothing about the contribution of these peoples to civilization, it fails to indicate the positive values of these cultures, it leaves the whole of Asia wrapped in deep shadow.'

A German critic complains of the German books that they paint world history as 'a rise of civilization from Egypt and the Greeks, etc. etc., to the advanced levels of the modern West': in fact, 'advance' is equated with 'western'. About an English book another German objects that 'the author makes no attempt to understand the attitude of the Chinese from any point of view other than the English one'; and this is echoed by an English critic of other English books on the same period—the mid-nineteenth century:

'In treating the Indian Mutiny authors rarely mention anything unfavourable to Britain, despite the ruthless reprisals said to have been taken. At best these will be described, for example, as involving "unnecessary cruelty and harshness", without the vivid detail given in respect of alleged Indian atrocities.'

The American books are apparently no better:

'The partiality to the British cause in the books analysed is found in the refusal to admit anything derogatory to the British administration. Very few books cite instances of repression and exploitation of the country by the alien government. On the contrary, it appears that whatever has been done under British auspices in India has been for the good of Indians.'

That was written by an Indian critic of American books. Of an English book another Indian complains that

'though in a subtle manner, the inferiority of the coloured peoples to Britons has been brought forth. . . . The coloured people are represented as very fearful of the British; at a mere sign from Livingstone the native slave-traders were so awe-stricken that they fled, leaving the slaves, even though they were armed and in number. It may not surprise us if the British children develop the idea that they can get the coloured people at their command under all circumstances.'

That takes the problem beyond the Orient into Africa; and it shows how even so slight a link as skin pigmentation may serve to unite Africans and Indo-Europeans in a common grievance against the complacent conceit of the whites.

On this general attitude of superiority to the easterners,

British books (according to their British critics) come out quite badly. While one author in particular is condemned as 'intolerant and patronizing in his references to "tyrants", "anarchy", "native hordes" and "brutality", and to "the natives, treacherous in the field and cowards out of it" ', many textbooks are said to contain

> 'the kind of comments which exalt "the long and honourable story of British rule in India", a view which in many respects might be endorsed, but which by itself might give a one-sided impression, especially when put in such terms as the following: "the people of India at last enjoyed the blessings—peace, order and justice—which they had been vainly seeking for 4,000 years".'

As the Indian critics say, it appears that whatever has been done under British auspices in India has been for the good of Indians, and 'it may not surprise us if British children develop the idea that they can get the coloured people at their command under all circumstances'.

It will perhaps be comforting to some of us to learn that things are little better behind the Iron Curtain. True, Russian books contain more about the East than books in countries which are not partly Asiatic, and lesser Communist countries have followed the Russian example. Czechoslovakia finds in eastern history much congenial material about castes, slave-owning classes, and exploitation. Hungary has a fair amount about China, whose native civilization, based as it is upon peasant culture and the multi-generation family home, is a fertile field for Communism. But an article in *Pravda* complains that, in the Soviet Republic of Uzbekistan at least,

> 'no serious scientific investigations have been made on some of the biggest eastern countries—China, India, Indonesia and others. . . . Thought should be given to

improving history teaching in secondary schools. Present time-tables allot quite inadequate time to the East.'

Criticisms of the American books by Americans may be allowed to sum up the problem and, more usefully perhaps, to suggest a solution:

'In all the textbooks examined students are led to see the culture, civilization and standards of living of the peoples of the East only through western eye-glasses, which means those of a highly industrialized civilization. This may, and does, create in boys and girls a feeling of superiority, and a patronizing, pitying attitude.'

A solution is suggested by the willingness of Americans to face the need, not merely to add something eastern to the already over-burdened syllabuses of history in schools and universities, but to consider how much traditional matter can be thrown overboard in the determination to make room for it:

'A considerable amount of material usually included about the United States and America seems much less significant than some major developments in Asiatic history which are ordinarily not included. . . . Topics which have been habitually included in history textbooks need to be re-examined to determine their pertinency.'

The Swiss reach the same conclusion with the usual Swiss eye to practical measures:

'All Swiss universities should establish chairs for the teaching of Asian history. Undergraduates studying for a history degree should be obliged to follow at least one course on Asian problems. . . . *Short* histories of Asia should be written . . . intended for the writers of textbooks, secondary school teachers, and university teachers.'

In other words the universities of the West are neglecting one of their primary functions so long as they (1) omit to provide access to the history and culture of three-quarters of the world, (2) continue to furnish a wholly inadequate body of information about the East, and (3) fail to produce teachers who can pass it on to the citizens of the future.

*   *   *

This problem of western misunderstanding of the East is quite different from the problem of misunderstanding among the western nations themselves. The western nations fail to understand one another, not because they are incapable of understanding but because they do not wish to understand. Even on the most recent periods, for which many of the documents are not yet available to historians, enough is known for us to form all but the most academic opinions. Whether Alsace is predominantly German or predominantly French is no longer a matter of research; the facts and statistics are all available; what causes international trouble is not German or French ignorance of the facts and figures, but different interpretations of the facts and figures by Germans and by French.

With misunderstanding between East and West things are altogether different. The man in the western street knows little about the East except what he thinks queer. Even the man in the western university knows little about the things which the East believes to be valuable. And even the man in the western university cannot go to, say, an eastern university for the knowledge which he lacks, as, for instance, a French or British or German or Russian university teacher can go to a Russian or German or British or French university. One of the most troublesome things about oriental history is that

Orientals themselves do not know it. In China, they have excellent chronological lists which a little industry can make most useful; but they had not, until recent years, anything approaching the accurate historiography of the West, and even in modern times they have not stored their documents, the raw material of history, as we in the West have done. In India, things are far worse. It may be true that there is no satisfactory history of China in Europe. It is certainly true that there is no satisfactory history of India in India or any-where else. A good deal of the best Hindu thought has no use whatever for history. History, they say, does not exist (which from one point of view is true enough); it is an illusion (which is pushing the idea farther than most westerners are willing to go); and therefore it is quite useless (which few western historians will accept at all, though one American millionaire has endorsed the Indian opinion less metaphysically with his much-quoted epigram, 'history is bunk'). Consequently, Indians have not written their history in any real western sense, and they have not preserved the documentary materials from which western scholars might do it for them. In China, there is very little ready-made history awaiting the question-ing westerner; in India, not only is there no ready-made history; history itself is discouraged if not taboo. Any scholar seeking to write a history of pre-European India that is satisfactory to westerners will have materials rather like the Homeric poems, and not much else, to work upon. All this, of course, does not mean that Indian history cannot be written; what it does mean is that pioneers in Indian history have to begin at the point which western historians had reached with their own history two or three hundred years ago. What India needs is not the kind of history which western universities have been turning out ever since the later nine-teenth century, but a Gibbon or a Macaulay who will use literary materials to write histories which men in the street will read, and later men in the universities will correct.

Of course, there has been a sporadic western interest in the East for at least two hundred years—ever since the East India Companies in their heyday began to turn India into an Eldorado, and since leaders of thought like Voltaire and Goldsmith began to supplement the fashionable *chinoiserie* of their day with a genuine intellectual curiosity about China. But Voltaire and Goldsmith were both more anxious, and better able, to prove Europe wrong than prove China right; and the India Companies were interested less in culture than in rupees. Since then, European Orientalists have flashed their torches on the East from time to time, and have illuminated this and that. Few of them, however, have managed to illuminate the vast East itself. They began with Sanskrit, and we were made to realize that in Sanskrit there were rich deposits of thought which the West had hardly conceived. But the rich deposits have remained largely unworked—or, if worked, rarely known or understood in the West except among specialists. Comparatively few educated Europeans have read at all carefully any of the Sanskrit classics, even in the translations which are now available. Yet as early as the eighteenth century we were assured by one of our most distinguished Orientalists (William Jones) that 'the Sanskrit language, whatever be its antiquity, is of a wonderful structure; more perfect than the Greek, more copious than the Latin, and more exquisitely refined than either'. Those of us who fear what might happen to the mind of Europe if Latin and Greek ceased to be staple subjects in our schools and universities, might pause to wonder what has already happened to the mind of Europe because we have never made staple school or university subjects of any of the rich languages and literatures of Asia. During the last five hundred years or so the regular study of the Latin (and, to a lesser extent, the Greek) language has shaped the thinking of Europe, and the regular study of Greek (and, to a lesser extent, Latin) literature has provided Europe with the basic material for its thought. What we should have lost without these regular disciplines we cannot measure. Western philosophy and poetry and art would have been wholly different. That, perhaps, will enable us to guess what we have lost already, not for five centuries but for twenty-five, through not knowing how to read and to comprehend what has been written in Chinese, or Sanskrit, or any of the Indian languages, or Persian or Arabic, 'one of the finest and most expressive forms of speech ever fashioned by the mind and tongue of man'.[1] 'Orientalism in this country has scarcely yet recovered from its damning and wholly un-informed indictment by Lord Macaulay, and we have lived to regret, in these late days, the lamentable results of an incomprehensible neglect of the cultural bonds forged with the peoples of Asia a century and a half since by a wiser generation of Englishmen.'[2]

The Eastern culture least unfamiliar to the West is that of the region which we used to call the Middle East—roughly the lands of the Arabs. Till the end of our 'Middle Ages' the Arabs were established well into the West. The best examples of their architecture, and two of their oldest and best universities, were in Spain. Their thought had filtered into the schools of western Europe, and the European school-men knew their favourite philosopher, Aristotle, through Latin translations of Arabic translations of the original Greek. By fighting Arabs in the Crusades western Europe had learned to construct pointed arches and minarets (which it called campaniles), and concentric castles equipped with machicolations, right-angled entrances and other Arab devices—besides sitting on sofas and dosing itself with rhubarb and senna. Of all these things we in the West are to some extent conscious.

[1] E. Atiyah: *The Arabs* (Pelican Books).
[2] Arberry: *British Orientalists* (Collins).

But we are far less conscious of the Arab claim to have been in the forefront of university development, or of the beauties of Arab poetry, 'the most distinguished and intimate creation of Arab aesthetic genius'. Few history specialists in the West have even heard of Ibn Khaldun, for whom it is claimed, by some western as well as eastern historians, that he was the greatest philosopher of history in any age or country. When it comes to modern times, our ignorance of Arab history seems in some ways yet more wanton. Who, for instance, would gather from most European writings that the greatest name in the modern history of Egypt is not Cromer or Kitchener, nor even Napoleon, but Mahomet Ali? It was he who started the stupendous advance of Egypt during the last hundred years, though British history books usually treat him as a mere adventurer if not a charlatan, whose chief title to fame is a stupid opposition to Palmerston. We hardly, even, realize who the Arabs are. How many English history books have made it clear to their readers that Egypt itself is an Arab country, and that Arabs stretch as far west as Morocco and further south than the Sahara? For that matter, how many English readers know that the Sudan is not merely 'Anglo-Egyptian', with a straight line of longitude for its western frontier, but a vast area reaching right across northern Africa almost to the Atlantic Ocean? We even use the wrong words for the religion of the Arabs. We call it 'Mohammedan', and dispute among ourselves how to spell it—not realizing that we should never spell it at all in any way, since to the people who call themselves Muslims the word Mohammedan is sacrilegious. To them it implies that 'Mohammedans' worship Mohammed, as 'Christians' worship Christ, and that offends a people whose monotheism is probably the strictest in the world.

Still, our intellectual gaucheries about the Arabs are as nothing compared with our gaucheries about the peoples and cultures of the Far East. The man in the street (and we ought never to forget that he was recently the boy in the school) is still hazy about the difference between an Indian and a Hindu, and still does not know that the word 'Chinaman' is an insult. He has never been told that, historically, neither pigtails nor pagodas are Chinese. He does not know what language Indians speak, or what gods the Chinese worship. He likes Chinese paintings and Japanese prints and Indian carpets, and Indian architecture (especially when it has been tidied up by the British); but he is content to leave mysterious all the essential cultural elements which have made India and China and the rest of the East what they are. No doubt this sort of vagueness is characteristic of men in the street everywhere. But it ought not to be characteristic of teachers in classrooms, and we ourselves are none too clear on many of the things we ought to know and to teach about the East.

Even our elementary geography is faulty. The Himalayas keep us right about India, but we do not know the northern frontiers of China. When we talk of the Malays we think of the inhabitants of one small peninsula formerly under British rule, and not of the millions of Malays stretching from the Indian Ocean into the Pacific. Our habit of labelling eastern territories by the name of the European peoples who for a time have conquered and held them vitiates our whole view of world geography and demography. 'Dutch' Indonesia, 'French' Indo-China, 'British' and 'Italian' Eritrea, 'British' and 'Portuguese' East and West Africa, the 'Belgian' Congo —all these names disguise the homogeneity of regions which European powers have parcelled into pieces governed separately upon European principles. The misconceptions generated by this tying of European labels upon non-European lands are themselves reflected throughout the geography and history books read by all Europeans, and they colour and falsify the ideas which Europeans cherish about Asia and Africa and their peoples. Look at any 'political' map of Africa: almost the whole of it is covered by colours which indicate nothing African at all, but only possession and exploitation by one or other of the European powers. Much the same thing is true of Asia, only there the European colouring is not nearly universal.

This geographical conception of the world so prevalent in the West is harmful enough, but it is far less mischievous than western misconceptions about the eastern religions. Religion cannot be left out of the history of the East, as it is so frequently left out of the history of the West. It is an astounding thing that nearly all English histories of the world omit any reference to what many English people regard as the most important event in the whole of world history. As our English books approach the turn from B.C. to A.D. they almost invariably fail to explain why there is any turn at all. They tell us plenty about Julius Caesar in the first century B.C., plenty about Claudius and Nero in the first century A.D., plenty about Augustus in the period bridging the two; but rarely anything whatever about Jesus Christ. He is relegated by the English books to some sphere of knowledge outside 'history'. English history books, which later go into details about the Christian Church, hardly ever explain how Christianity came into existence, or mention its religious meaning for mankind. Like the Russian books on the Reformation, English history books treat Christianity as a matter merely of institutions and organization, never as a matter of the spirit. That may be convenient, in these days when conviction is lacking, and Protestant churches are almost empty. In Catholic lands, where the churches are never empty, they do not omit Jesus Christ from their historical accounts of Christianity, and fewer children are given the impression that the events of the New Testament are really too suspect to be put into a history book.

One of the first things historians have to learn about the history of the East is that it will not do to omit religion. In the lives of most Asians, religion is a far more commonplace and vital thing than it is in the lives of most Europeans and Americans. Moreover, eastern religion is not the freakish thing many westerners imagine it to be. The important features of the eastern faiths are not fakirs and yoga and badly run festivals, or crackers or incense-sticks or ancestor-worship. They are not even the innumerable shrines to this, that, or the other of thousands of gods. What matters most in the eastern religions is their ethical and spiritual sincerity. Of course most Asians fail to observe the precepts of their faiths, as most westerners fail to observe theirs. But the best adherents of the Asian religions are not less sincere than the most religious people in the West, and they regard their religions as equally true.

This matter of the truth of religious beliefs needs to be faced by most western historians far more seriously than hitherto. There are, of course, plenty of unbelievers in the East as well as in the West, and their unbelief extends to western as well as to eastern religious doctrines. That, however, is not typical of Asia. Asia believes in religion—even in religions; the difficulty is not that Asians will not believe in Christianity, but that they believe in it too easily. Their idea of religious tolerance is far less passive than ours. It is not confined to an absence of government interference; it deprecates all non-official interference including, of course, missionary activity, which it regards as a form of religious intolerance. Tolerance in the East is positive—it includes the willingness to believe that other religions are good, even if not so good as one's own. They are quite willing, therefore, to credit the miraculous in Christianity. The miracles of Christian tradition are very similar to the miracles of their own religions; and even the divinity of Jesus Christ rests on claims in many ways identical with those made for the Lord Buddha. They therefore tend to accept the divinity of Jesus on the same level as the divinity of Buddha, and when they find Christians refusing to reciprocate, they count it for religious intolerance. Indeed, Christianity is regarded in the East as having been the most persecuting of all religions. Even Islam, and still more the non-proselytizing religions of Asia, have not persecuted for religious reasons—or so at least they claim, and it is a claim with which historians must reckon. Some of their rulers, like the European Henry VIII or Charles V, have permitted persecution for political reasons: few have been like Henry VIII's daughter, and her husband Charles V's son, in encouraging persecution for the saving of souls.

Another matter in which the books of the West, and in particular perhaps our history books, are thought to wrong the religions of the East, is the worship of 'idols'. In this we are the victims of our own etymology. The word 'idol', which after all means much the same as 'statue', carries in the mouths of Christians and Jews an undertone of sinful worship. In the West few people see any sin in a statue: in the East few educated people would admit that when they 'bow down to wood and stone' they are worshipping it. In the East as in the Catholic West it is only the most ignorant who worship images, and they do it through ignorance. The best Asians, like the best Europeans, when they bow before an image or an altar, are worshipping not the image or the altar, but the divinity behind it. Yet in Protestant Europe the tradition of our hymns dies hard, and the misunderstandings they have fostered for a century or more are still with us, reflected into our history books.

It is not merely in hagiology, however, that western historians and others misrepresent the religions of the East. They are equally biased in their treatment of eastern doctrine, and with less excuse, since the eastern scriptures are available

for us to read, if we will only read them. In the West we know
that the basic principle of all ethics is the duty to love your
neighbour as yourself. None of us manages to do this, but we
accept the principle. Many of us are obtuse enough to imagine
that it is a purely Christian principle, though we should know
that the New Testament quotes it from the Old, and that it is
therefore Jewish. But it is not merely Jewish. At just about
the time when this Golden Rule was being written into
Leviticus, it was being spoken and written into the scriptures
of the other great religions as well. 'Thou shalt love thy
neighbour as thyself,' says *Leviticus*, somewhere about 500
B.C. At much the same epoch Confucius put it in a form
which some of his followers manage to get into a single
Chinese character: 'Do not do to others what you would not
like done to yourself.' 'Let a man overcome anger by love and
evil by good,' say the Buddhist scriptures. For the Hindu,
'the true worshipper of Vishnu is he who knows and feels
another's woes as his own'. A little later Socrates or Plato
introduced the principle into Europe: 'We ought not to repay
evil with evil, or do wrong to any man, whatever the cost.'
And a thousand years afterwards it reached the *Koran*: 'Turn
away evil with good.' Some time or other, too, it got into the
Tao Te Ching, the chief book of the Taoist scriptures: 'Requite
hatred with virtue . . . Gentleness overcomes strength . . . the
sage puts himself last and finds himself in the first place.' And
Taoism, as the West is now coming to recognize, has been
an even more potent influence on Chinese conduct than
Confucianism. Confucianism, which is not a religion because
it knows no gods, has been the code of the intellectuals. The
ordinary Chinese has failed to live up to its strait-laced
Victorianism, and has found the *Tao*—'the Way, the Truth,
and the Life'—easier to follow. That, we are now assured
by sinologists, is a historical revision long overdue in the
West.

For centuries now the West has regarded the East (all the East) as though it were one—a unity of religious mysticism beyond any western understanding. We have contrasted the mystical East with the practical West; like Toynbee, we have felt secure in the belief that 'a mechanical penchant is as characteristic of our western civilization as an aesthetic penchant was of the Hellenic, or a religious penchant was of the Indic and the Hindu'. Many western historians (even those who distrust Toynbee most) would accept that verdict. Apparently it is untrue. While our professional historians have been repeating platitudes about the unpractical East a distinguished bio-chemist, a Fellow of the Royal Society, has been looking at the facts. 'All such valuations of East and West are built on insecure foundations,' says Needham,[1] and he is devoting seven vast volumes to details about the mechanical penchant of the civilization of China.

At the root of our misconceptions about the history of Chinese science, and of all eastern science, is our failure to appreciate the science of their thought. Philosophers from Socrates and before to Descartes and after have committed us in the West to a trust in logic, and syllogistic logic at that. There is precious little logic, and hardly a syllogism at all, in the characteristic thought of the East. Indians, it is true, during two centuries of British influence learnt to think along Cartesian lines; but even for them this kind of thinking remains a foreign importation. 'The Chinese,' says a distinguished Indian historian, 'have not been influenced by Cartesian logic. . . . It is difficult to find a Chinese logician, and Chinese thought in the past has inclined to be more fluid, poetic and intuitive'. Certainly the Taoist literature of China has been 'fluid, poetic and intuitive', if the Confucian literature has not. So have all the older works in the literature of India. Throughout the whole of history the

[1] *Science and Civilization in China,* I, p. 241.

thinking of most of the East has been not logical but intuitive; it does not step warily in our western manner; it jumps, and usually it lands right. Or rather (for any such concrete metaphor must be mistaken) it ripples along from idea to idea, until the full conception emerges almost without conscious effort. If western philosophers complain that this kind of thinking is inaccurate and unsystematic, the eastern reply is simple—life and conduct themselves are inaccurate and unsystematic, and eastern thought is therefore truer to life than thought constricted by the artificial rules of the West.

This ignorance about the way eastern peoples think has always warped our western conceptions of eastern conduct, including the past conduct which we call history. And our ignorance extends not only to the way they think about their own affairs, but to the way they think about matters in which we have always been confident of our own superiority— science and technology. In this confidence we have been simply wrong. We have not known that throughout history, until our own Industrial Revolution, the East has been ahead of the West even in science and technology. No doubt we have been aware that the medieval Arabs were good at astronomy and astrology, and were responsible for occasional contributions to pure mathematics, such as 'Arabic' numerals and the notion of zero. We are less certain about these things than we were, because we are now told that most of them (even Arabic figures) are not Arabic at all, but probably Indian or Chinese. As far as India is concerned, we have no authority for knowing how far these claims are true—Indians have been as indifferent to the history of their science as to the rest of their history. Even for India, however, new methods of research are giving us glimpses we have been denied hitherto. In the science of language, they say, India led the ancient world; in the fourth century B.C. India produced the first of all scientific grammars. Her metal-founding and artistry were better than anything in the West throughout the Middle Ages. And in fact, even before the Middle Ages, not only metallurgy but mining, civil engineering, medicine and chemistry were all among the sciences being regularly practised in India.

Moslems have been less indifferent to history than Hindus, and less silent about their own past achievements. That is why we know much more about the Arabian than the Indian contributions to medieval science. By the fourteenth century A.D. Samarkand had the finest astronomical observatory in the world. Early in the twelfth century Muslim scientists were talking about the gravitational pull of the earth, and about the circulation of the blood four hundred years before Harvey. They were operating for cataract in the time of Chaucer. More practical still, they were a thousand years ahead of Europe in using the collar and breast-strap harnesses which enabled them to employ draught-oxen without throttling them. Details like these are hardly known in the West, perhaps because they are largely disregarded by such historians as there are in the East. Moreover, many of these technical accomplishments are disputed among the Asian peoples themselves, and there is not as yet enough evidence of the sort the West is prepared to accept to enable us to decide between their rival claims. But together they go to support Needham's assertion that in technology and science 'Asia was greatly in advance of Europe from the earliest times till about the sixteenth century A.D.'.

To what extent this is true of India and the Middle East we may not know until after lifetimes of research. But at least one lifetime of research has already shown that it is true of China. Needham's monumental history of Chinese science and civilization has established itself, before being half published, as the most revolutionary book on Chinese history so far

written in English. It has put all western study of China on
an entirely new footing—though the work of scholars like
Grousset has made it all less surprising to Frenchmen than to
Englishmen. It recognizes that science and civilization in
China are inextricably intermingled with philosophy and
ethics and even religion. And yet, throughout, the emphasis
is on technical achievement—Chinese history is a pageant,
not of processions to pagodas, nor of the failure of bookish
examinees to run politics on bookish lines, but of constant
technical progress in all directions. It is exceedingly difficult
to choose examples from a book of 3000 to 4000 pages, packed
with evidence from all branches of science and technology.
If civilization means comfort and convenience, then the
Chinese had oilskin raincoats hundreds of years B.C., and at
least one book for luxury travellers about 1000 A.D.: 'Don't
forget your raincoat, your medicine chest, plenty of spare
clothes, a box of preserved food supplies and tea, paper, ink,
scissors, a rhyming dictionary and a lute, chessboard and
chessmen, and a box for books bought on the journey.' If
civilization means mechanical devices, then the Chinese had
mechanical clocks (driven by the first chain-drive in history)
with a fully developed escapement by the eighth century A.D.,
and slide-calipers in the ninth. Gearing for machinery, with
v-toothed wheels, they knew 2000 years ago. They used
iron chains for suspension bridges in the eighth century
—Europe adopted them in the eighteenth. Another anticipa-
tion by a thousand years of our Industrial Revolution was the
water-powered spinning machine. Clockwork-driven tele-
scopes, which reached Europe during the nineteenth century,
were known in China seven centuries earlier. They were 'a
people who were the finest bronze-founders of antiquity, and
who made cast-iron thirteen centuries before Europeans'. In
medicine, they were using general anaesthesia by A.D. 300
(sixteen hundred years before J. Y. Simpson), and inoculation

D

for smallpox by 1100 (600 years before Lady Mary Wortley Montagu). And in the thirteenth century they had in Sung Tzhu 'the founder of forensic medicine not only in China, but in the whole world'.

In the history of farming, too, some of their achievements will stagger students of our Agricultural Revolution. They had seed-drills in the third century A.D., fourteen hundred years before Tull. At about the same period they were already familiar with entomological pest-control on lines not used in Europe till the nineteenth century. And the wheelbarrow, which revolutionized most gardening and much farming in Europe in the seventeenth century, was a common Chinese convenience in the third.

There is the same tale to tell about mathematics and pure science. Apart from claims (such as the discovery of zero) disputed with India and other eastern lands, there is their invention of a decimal system about 300 B.C., and a little later their familiarity with negative quantities. In the science of light they were the superiors of the Greek contemporaries of Aristotle. They did for algebra, it is claimed, what the Greeks did for geometry: and quite early they evolved 'an organic philosophy of nature closely resembling that which modern science has been forced to adopt after three centuries of mechanical materialism'.

In fact, with the Chinese—as with most of the East— science never ceased, as it did in Europe a century or more ago, to be 'Natural Philosophy'. The study of science was never divorced from the study of thought in general, including religion. For instance, we are told that Wang Yang-Ming anticipated Kant's categorical imperative by three centuries, and that Lu Hsiang Shan anticipated by six centuries Kant's affirmation of the subjectivity of space and time. And as if to show themselves more 'modernist' still in philosophy, their psychologists were airing the conception of sin as a curable disease at the time of our Reformation, when Europe's most conspicuous remedy for sin was burning at the stake.

All this will seem to most Englishmen a very un-English kind of history. Even today, more than a hundred years after Buckle, more than sixty after Green, most English historians still treat history as though it were mainly past politics. That could never be true of the far East, where politics has been a very different affair. To the average Chinese throughout the ages, politics has meant little more than a distant shadowy emperor, the need to square his tax-collectors, and periodic descents by war-lords and their bands to ruin the crops for anything from a season to a decade. Even if there could be a political history of China it would have to concern itself less with what we call politics, than with what we used to call political economy. While we in Europe have been struggling for a couple of generations to make our history less political and more social, in China history could never be anything else. There, progress in government has meant, not, as in Europe, the achievement, exercise and debasement of the franchise, but things with a much more modern sound: Land Nationalization in the first century A.D.; old-age pensions in the fourteenth; and during the seventeenth, in Wang Ch'uan Shan, one who is described as 'a forerunner of Marx and Engels'.

That is why those who fear or desire the growth of Communism in China would do well to study, not the speeches of Mao Tse Tung, but social history. It is not merely that a kind of Communism could be preached in the seventeenth century by Wang Ch'uan Shan. From very early times they had, even more than medieval Europe, the natural communism of the common fields—which, like the common fields of Europe, were partly feudal as well as partly communal. And of course there is the fundamental communism of their family life. 'There are many traditional elements of Chinese thought and ideology which may well be harmonized with the outlook of Marxism—e.g. the position of the family. The *family idea*, based in China on group solidarity, has shown itself adaptable to Communist requirements, and not antagonistic to them. The efforts at collectivization and great public works, on the basis of such solidarity, fit in with the social tradition of local community service.' Those are the words of an Indian and a Frenchman, in the UNESCO report on the treatment of the East in western textbooks. As far back as history can see, the Chinese family has consisted, not of one man and his wife and their children, but of generations of kinsmen with their women and children living in a single home—a home where, as the young men marry, it seems more convenient to add to the buildings than to permit the family fragmentation with which we are familiar in the West. All this is natural Communism, not synthetic, like that of Marx and Engels, or even Wang Ch'uan Shan. The soil of China is already fertile in a Chinese Communism, whether or not the Soviets succeed in superimposing upon it Communism of a Russian sort. The West may one day find itself worried, not because China is becoming Communist, but because Communism is becoming Chinese.

Thus, even in politics, we of the political West need to think ourselves out of our historical obsessions in order to grasp the thought-processes of the East, and the social contexts by which those thought-processes are conditioned. And not only in social and political history. Eastern culture in all its forms tends to elude the western mind, unless the western mind makes a desperate effort to break through what has been called the thought-barrier. Indian sculpture seems to us incomprehensibly over-elaborate; and yet its over-elaboration is as sincere and expressive as that of European Gothic. Chinese paintings seem sketchy; and so they are. They are

sketches, but profound sketches. How many European painters could boast of producing a masterpiece in five minutes?
That is what Chinese painters have done, because they aim, not
at the sort of detail which culminated here in the Pre-
Raphaelites, but at the rapid embodiment of fleeting ideas.
They catch the mood of the passing moment; they paint it,
almost in the moment itself, and the painting is always good,
often great, sometimes superlative.

In the history of the East such things are far more important
than anything political. In the story of the eastern past,
politics do not matter much—not even the politics of military
conquest. The West has more valuable things to learn from
eastern history than how to wage wars or govern states. We
have done that sort of thing better ourselves.

There are some things, however, which we have not always
done better ourselves, though we have always thought so. If
the word 'civilization' means what it says, China was more
'civilized' than Europe for the whole of the millennium and a
half which elapsed between the decay of the Roman Empire
and the beginning of the Industrial Revolution. Throughout
that period Chinese cities were bigger and better than European cities, and most of the elements which go to make what
we call 'civilization' were more advanced among the Chinese
than they were in the West. For one thing, there was, in the
seventh century A.D., a regulation that every city should have
its own Medical Officer of Health. The communications of the
Chinese Empire remained, unlike the communications of
Europe, as good as those of the Roman Empire had been.
Their commercial centres were busier than those of Europe,
and the goods they sold were of better workmanship. Moreover, they knew the civilized pleasures of beauty and leisure.
Of the aesthetic as well as the financial value of their paintings
and their porcelain, European collectors have been fully aware
for generations. About their music we know perhaps less than

we do about the music of the Greeks—but even that is more than past European historians have realized. We know that they had something like a lute two to three hundred years B.C., though we cannot know what it played. At any rate, they interested themselves in the sympathetic resonance induced in one lute when another was struck; and they even had a well-tempered scale (based, we are told, on the twelfth root of two) a hundred years before Bach was born.

Then there is their poetry. It lies hidden, of course, behind the barrier of language as well as the barrier of our historical ignorance. Most of us can know it only in translations, and translations into a kind of prose no more like the original than our Psalter is like the poetry of the original Hebrew Psalms. Yet beauty shines clear even through barriers as insurmountable as these. Where in Wordsworth could one find anything to surpass that combination of lyrical beauty with emotional delight in Nature which abounds in the poems of the T'ang, and to a lesser extent of the Sung, dynasties? No doubt, as the Chinese civilization ripened towards decay, their poetry, like ours, became more sophisticated and cynical. But there is enough Chinese poetry, as there is enough Indian poetry, magnificent even in translation, to make nonsense of the complacent boast of Macaulay, who damned Indian literature without having read it, and claimed that the literature extant in his day in English was 'of far greater value than all the literature which 300 years ago was extant in all the languages of the world together'.

Around Chinese poetry there gathered, as usual, other kinds of literature and their ancillary publications. Unlike the Indians, the Chinese wrote histories, including a current contemporary history which ran, like our Anglo-Saxon Chronicle, for centuries—and whose chronology is said to be at least as reliable as most contemporary chronologies in the West. Writers of the T'ang also compiled records of local topography comparable with Domesday Book. In Lu Chia and his work on the rise and fall of states there was even a Chinese Toynbee in the second century B.C. By the ninth century A.D., besides paper and printing they had a sort of shorthand. As for works of reference, Chinese encyclopaedias make the *Encyclopaedia Britannica* look like a pocket-book. They were being produced from the ninth century onwards. In the eighteenth and nineteenth centuries the most up-to-date of them was extended to 1700 volumes, and that was nothing to an encyclopedia of the fifteenth century which reached 11,000 volumes. A good deal of their contents have appeared nonsense to European critics; but then no doubt most of the literature of fifteenth century Europe would seem nonsense to a modern Chinese.

'A man shall ever see, that, when ages grow to civility and elegancy, men come to build stately, sooner than to garden finely; as if gardening were the greater perfection.' If this criterion of Bacon's for civilized maturity is sound, the Chinese come out with flying colours. There is the artistry of those miniature gardens with which the overcrowded cities of Asia have so often been compelled to content themselves. But by gardening Bacon meant landscape gardening in units of thirty-five acres or so: and on that scale the spacious estates of rich Chinese for centuries past have exhibited a 'civility and elegancy' beside which the achievements of Lenôtre seem simple, and Capability Brown not much more than an accomplished hedger and ditcher.

Yet when all is said and done it is neither for their supremely Augustan elegance, nor for their exploration of the deeper mysteries of the spirit, that we of the modern West need to study the real history of the East. And if it comes to that those are not the reasons why easterners wish us to study their history. Their more advanced thinkers have already reached the stage where they are inclined to depreciate the foundations of their own cultures, and follow Japan in going western. The West has remained ignorant of the cultures of the East, but the East has had the cultures of the West forced upon it by musket and cannon, and now her peoples are resolved to try musket and cannon and the rest of western paraphernalia for themselves. Consequently, in our own day, the peoples of the East are asking us to judge them by western standards. They are beginning to be prouder of their modern industries than of their ancient philosophies. They would like us to look away from their fabled mysticisms and pay more attention to their Five-Year Plans and their blue-prints, and to the facility with which they can adopt and adapt completely western expedients like democracy and Communism.

Thus the western history books have still a long way to go in their appreciation of the East. We have first to discard completely our already moribund sense of superiority, then to estimate the East by what it has been in itself, rather than by what it has done in resistance or submission to the West. Finally, when we have understood how to learn from its philosophies and its arts, ancient and modern, we have to forget the Shalimar and the Temple of Heaven, our notions of Nirvana and of the correct behaviour of the Confucian gentleman; we have even to put away our copies of the *Bhagavadgita* and the *Tao Te Ching*, and visualize an East which is not only as eastern as it has always been, but which is rapidly becoming western in ways the West has never known.

5

European History: What Is It?

FROM 1953 to 1958 the Council of Europe held six annual
conferences on 'The European Idea in The Teaching of
History'. Till now, it was felt, the Idea of Europe has
been conspicuously lacking in our history books. Our histories of England are about England, not about one county
after another. Histories of France are about France, not about
the evolution of the departments; even histories of Germany
and of the United States are about Germany or the United
States, not about the separate states, once independent, from
which united Germany and the United States were formed.
But our histories of Europe are not about Europe. Examine
any book, in almost any language, which calls itself a European History, and you will find that it is not a history of
Europe at all: it is a history, or rather piecemeal histories, of
the states or peoples which comprise Europe. There will be
chapters on the history of France, and Germany, and Britain,
and so on; but few if any chapters on Europe as a whole.
Although there will, no doubt, be accounts of the Catholic
Church and Feudalism and one or two other features common to all the states of Europe, not even the Holy Roman
Empire usually figures as a continental phenomenon—
especially in Germany, which goes out of its way to emphasize
that it is the 'Holy Roman Empire of the German Nation'.
The idea of Europe as a unit is hardly ever presented to young

people of Europe, trying to learn the history of the past which has made them and their continent what they are.

That is why the Council of Europe felt it essential to take steps towards encouraging, in the history lessons of the schools of Europe, this 'idea' of Europe. After all, if there are things in the English past which every Englishman ought to know because they have created his national environment for him, there are things (perhaps far more) which every European ought to know, because they have created our continental environment.

But what is this continental environment? What are the things whose history we should know because we are Europeans? Once that problem is propounded, difficulties begin to flow in fast. Englishmen know what they mean by England, at any rate considered as a territorial unity. We are a group of islands, and land's end, wherever it occurs, is the end of our land. But no such criterion can be applied to Europe. We western Europeans fail to appreciate this because we know that Land's End, and Finisterre, and the rest, are in fact the territorial limits of Europe in the West. At the other end, however, things are not so simple. And this can be less easily realized by us British in our tight little island than by French and Germans (who are never sure, for example, whether Alsace is German or French) and Danes (who have their doubts about Holstein) and Italians (who become confused with other nations in Switzerland and the Tyrol), and even Spaniards, since there are in fact bits of the Pyrenees which hardly know whether they are Spanish or French. And if in the West Europe has frontier uncertainties of this kind, what about places like Poland and the Balkan States, whose frontiers have been shifting to and fro throughout the whole of history—and are shifting still?

Yet these frontier problems of the separate states are trivial compared with the problem of the eastern frontier of the continent of Europe as a whole. What is that frontier? Most Englishmen will glibly answer 'the Urals'. But in fact a very large part of eastern Europe has no Urals; there is a gap of about fifteen degrees of latitude between the southern end of the Urals and the south of Greece—a distance about as far as from London to Iceland or Algiers. At the Caucasus there is, indeed, something like a 'frontier' between Europe and Asia. But from Urals to Caucasus is 1400 miles of lowland—some of it (perhaps ten or twenty times as much as the whole of Holland) below sea level—with no sort of natural frontier anywhere. If you live at the north end of the Caspian Sea, is your house in Europe or Asia? Probably none of the people who do live there has the least notion.

In any case, by no means all the atlases will confirm our glib judgment that the Urals themselves constitute a frontier. Atlases published in different countries give different frontiers for eastern Europe; a good many of the historical atlases, British and foreign, dodge the problem by giving no frontiers at all in that region. It is, of course, absurd to imagine that two families, living on opposite slopes of hills no higher than those of Wales, are therefore in different continents—still more absurd if they live on opposite sides of the swampy valley of the River Ural. Whatever atlases may say, the two families do in fact live in the same district; that district is an economic no man's land, and no man knows whether it is Europe or Asia.

Every man, however, knows that it is all Russia. That is another of the absurdities which we cherish about Europe. We talk of 'Russia in Europe' and 'Russia in Asia': but politically as well as economically there are no such things. There is just 'Russia', and it is nonsense to treat inhabitants of Leningrad and Vladivostock as though they were not really members of the same political and cultural community. With Russia bestriding the wide world like a Colossus, who are we petty men to maintain that she has one foot in Europe and the other in Asia? The conception of Russia is still real, although she has advanced in modern times from the Baltic to the Pacific. The conceptions of Europe and Asia are not nearly so real; they were hardly real in the Middle Ages. They are far less real now that one European power has spread as far east as China, while other European powers, colonizing westwards, have planted between Atlantic and Pacific a civilization usually regarded as much more European than that of the Soviet Union.

Yet Russia, though perhaps the most intractable of Europe's problems, and though her territory in Asia is far larger than the whole of Europe put together, nevertheless has strong claims to be regarded as an essential part of the European community. Not only is she as Slavonic and as Christian as Poland or Czechoslovakia; she is a greater Slavonic nation than either, and in her own eyes at least her Christianity is more orthodox than that of Rome. True, there has never been a time during the last five hundred years when Russia has not looked and developed towards the East; but Peter the Great europeanized at least the upper strata of her social system, and built for her a capital city on European lines, looking towards the Atlantic Ocean. Eastwards, she had more room to expand, and little effective opposition. Westwards, she constantly met opposition very effective indeed. Yet she always looks, with a nostalgia all the more acute for being Slav, beyond the Vistula and even the Oder to those lands along the Elbe which were Slavonic a thousand years ago, until they were absorbed in a German *Drang nach Osten* begun in the eighth century by a Teutonic Charlemagne and completed in the sixteenth by the Grand Master of the Teutonic Order. In our own day, Russia has undone the history of the last millennium; the Oder, even the Elbe, are once again under the sway of the Slav. The edifice reared so painfully by the greatest German statesmen from Charle-magne to Bismarck, has been toppled over. The Slavs are back where they were in the Dark Ages.

Here, in fact, we strike the reverse of the problem of Europe's eastern frontier; and here, if anywhere, Germany can justly complain that she has been misunderstood by the West. Complain she does, vociferously: but of course throughout recent times Germany has cried 'wolf' so often and so persistently, and has tumbled so readily into self-pity when she has met with the same troubles and treatment as other nations, that we in the West can perhaps excuse our-selves for failing to take her seriously when we really ought. Because we are in the West, and because Germany has fought us all, we tend to forget that her main preoccupations are in the East. Germany's chief worry has always been not Britain, or America, or even France, but Russia. The principal German problem is not western, but eastern. Across the Rhine, modern Germany has constantly faced frustration, political, economic and social: across the Vistula she has always faced death. And now, in our days, death has over-taken her, and we in the West, though we were in at the kill, barely realize what has happened. Germany—the Germany of the Kaisers, of Bismarck, of Frederick the Great—is dead; whether it can be resurrected, the twentieth century may never know. The Slav peril, which has haunted German minds since before Charlemagne, and against which Charle-magne was only the first of a long line of German statesmen to build bulwarks, has swamped her at last. Germany—the Germany whose chief city was once Vienna and later Berlin—exists no longer. For at least three centuries German Kings and Kaisers and Chancellors have striven strenuously to unite their country, to restore the old Holy Roman Empire of the German Nation, building, like Nehemiah's men, with a trowel in one hand and a sword in the other. They succeeded:

for fifty, perhaps seventy-five, years there was a German Empire again. Now it is gone. Germany is once again piecemeal, and the West is beginning to see that Charlemagne and the Teutonic Knights and Frederick the Great and Bismarck and the Kaiser and even Hitler were right—destroy Germany, and western Europe opens its eastern gates to the all-pervading Slav.

That, at least, is how German historians have always seen the situation: and nowadays many French, English and even American historians are beginning to see it that way too. Whether or no they are right depends not on the policy of this or that German government, but on whether or no the Slavs are 'European'—and not only the Slavs, but the Germans themselves. In those eastern regions the 'idea of Europe' involves a double question—are the Russians, and are the Germans, really 'European'? We are accustomed to say that the triple foundations of Europe are Christianity, Greece and Rome. If so, how far have Russia and Germany been built on those foundations? Both countries have been Christian in their different ways. Neither of them, however, was ever included in the Roman Empire. Arminius, the first of a long succession of German generals to throw back an enemy from the Westphalian Gate, destroyed more than the lost legions of Augustus. He also destroyed Germany's chance of becoming Romanized like the rest of the western-land. Medieval Germany formed part of the Roman Church without ever having formed part of the Roman Empire. No wonder medieval and modern Germans have found it difficult to understand, and be understood by, medieval and modern Frenchmen and Italians and Spaniards and even Englishmen.

From this point of view, paradoxically enough, the effect of history has been to make Russia more 'European' than Germany. Germany, like the rest of us in the West, had to wait till the Renaissance for the direct impact of Hellenism.

Russia, on the other hand, was in direct contact with Greece all through the Middle Ages. For her, the capital of the Roman Empire was not Rome but Byzantium—which was, in fact, the capital of the Roman Empire for more than twice as long as Rome. Moreover, throughout the Middle Ages and since, Russia has been a member of the Greek Church, sharing an English litany's distrust of 'the bishop of Rome and all his detestable enormities', and the belief that Papists are heretics. If Russian history has had less of Rome than history in the West, it has had a double portion of Greece to make up the deficiency. History has created the West from materials Greek and Roman and Christian. Russia, though not Roman, it has made Christian and doubly Greek. Germany was equally Christian, and Greek after the Renaissance, but never Roman. On this reasoning the 'idea of Europe' should include Russia rather than Germany. That notion is patently absurd. The problem needs to be approached from a different direction.

Where the history of culture has failed us, can historical geography help us to an answer? Here again the evidence is confusing. Historical geography has never fixed an eastern frontier for Europe. In this matter we of the West are the victims of our own misconceptions. We have a neat desire to end every war with a restoration or a modification of the *status quo*. Consequently in 1945 we found ourselves puzzled to powerlessness by Russia's insistence that east of the Elbe there had never been a *status quo*. To Slavonic notions of history, Prussia and everything as far west as the Oder is Slavonic land; and even the area between Oder and Elbe has always been debatable ground. It was debated among the barbarian nations when they were surging westwards into the collapsing Roman Empire. It was debated when Charlemagne reversed the Slavonic tide in the eighth century, and when the Teutonic Knights, among others, continued this German *Drang nach Osten*. It was debated between Charles XII and

Peter the Great, and between Catherine the Great and
Frederick the Great. It was debated by Napoleon in 1812 and
by Russian Czars throughout the nineteenth century, from
the Greek War of Independence through the Crimea in the
fifties and the Balkans in the seventies to the war of 1914–19.
In our own days it was debated between Stalin and Hitler.
This time the debate has gone decisively in favour of the
Slavs, who have had no compunction in putting back the
curtain (not so iron after all) between Teuton and Slav to
where it was a thousand years ago. The whirligig of time has
brought its revenges. Whether it will bring in yet another
counter-revenge remains for the future to see. Meantime,
historians can continue to discuss in their academic circles the
whereabouts of Europe's eastern frontier throughout history.

For an 'idea of Europe' the history of the eastern frontier
has been so unsettling that it dwarfs all the others. Yet
Europe has her historical frontier problems not only in the
north and east, but south-east and south-west, and even
north-west. Here, in our north-western islands, our allegiance
to Europe has always been suspect. Perhaps it is absurd to
suggest that Britain is not European; yet other Europeans
often express their doubts about it. Their present exaspera-
tion because we will not join in forming a European community is matched by our own insularity in the past, as well
as the present. In so far as we pride ourselves on that insularity
we are holding ourselves aloof from the continent of Europe.
In fact, foreigners do find themselves puzzled by our habit of
referring to 'the Continent' as a place to which Britons can
go, as though we were not there already. And foreign historians are equally puzzled to note that hardly any of our so-called
'histories of Europe' contain any chapters about Britain. Even
our 'British histories' make it abundantly clear that we have
closer ties with lands in all the other continents than with any
country or people on the European mainland. After all, most

citizens of the British Commonwealth live outside Europe, and it is still true that only the minority are white-skinned. Though few believe it, many Britons, historians and others, often act as though the north-west frontier of Europe were the Straits of Dover.

There is an almost equal uncertainty in the south-west. The Pyrenees make a formidable frontier, and there or thereabouts was, in fact, the frontier between Christendom and Islam throughout much of the Middle Ages. Though the Roman Empire managed to penetrate the Iberian Peninsula from the south, the Holy Roman Empire failed to hold it from the north. Even through modern times Spain has been, like Britain, a country apart. In our own days she has taken her stand against the sort of democracy which has set its seal upon the rest of western Europe: and until 1958 Spain, like Russia (but unlike Turkey and Iceland), remained hostile to the Council of Europe.

Still, it is not in the west but in the south-east that we must look for a European frontier problem comparable in difficulty to that of the Slav-German marchlands. In the south-east, history has to find a place in Europe for Byzantium during the Middle Ages and for Turkey in modern times. Byzantium surely was always European. Yet if that is so, must we not include in medieval Europe all Asia Minor and much of Syria, if not of Africa—all integral parts of the Byzantine Empire? Like the Roman Empire which it claimed to continue, the Empire of Byzantium stretched right round the Mediterranean. After all, Asia Minor itself was called 'Rome' by the Saracens, and has been re-christened 'Europa Minor' by a modern Englishman. Byzantium in its early days could almost echo the claim of Pompey to have pushed the Roman Empire as far as the Euphrates—yet the empire which Pompey bequeathed to the Caesars was indubitably 'European'.

For modern times, the problem is reversed. Nowadays it is a question, not of the penetration of the Levant by Europeans, but of the penetration of Europe by Levantines. Does Europe today include Turkey? If Byzantium and Constantinople were European, what of Istanbul? And if Istanbul is European, what of Ankara? Does the character of modern Turkey, like that of medieval Byzantium, demand that Europe shall include Asia Minor? Nearly all of modern Turkey is in what we call Asia—and yet Turkey is in the Council of Europe. In any case, it is hardly sensible to suggest that Istanbul and Ankara are in different continents. They certainly share the same culture, and the Turks themselves insist that that culture is 'European'.

Turkey is a special case, and it deserves special consideration. The Turks are the latest-comers into Europe, and nearly all the non-Turkish Europeans still regard them as outsiders. Italians, Gauls, Germans, Spaniards, English, Scandinavians, and the rest have dwelt in Europe for at least 2000 years. The Turks have been here for less than 600. That, however, is by no means decisive. The Turks have been in Europe for much longer than the Americans have been in America; so that length of tenure may be held to tell rather for than against the Turkish case. But in fact that case rests upon quite different evidence; evidence not only of the fluctuations of Europe's south-eastern frontier throughout history, but of cultural affinities. The Turks may have been in modern Europe for six centuries at most; but they have been well inside the old Roman Empire for over nine centuries. Moreover, as they advanced into the crumbling Byzantine Empire they took over many of its traditions, so that in late medieval and early modern times the Ottoman Empire was merely (in the words of a Greek historian of the University of Athens) 'the Byzantine Empire in Turkish hands'.

Western Europe was not conscious of this at the time, and

has never been conscious of it since. To the older inhabitants of Europe the Ottoman came, not as the preserver of a Roman culture, but as the Terrible Turk; and the Terrible Turk he remained till the time of Gladstone and after. The older Europeans met the Turks chiefly in war, or in a commerce which was largely warlike. Turkish historians claim that this has entirely warped western ideas about Turkish history. Western textbooks have always chronicled the Turkish wars, and have usually ignored Turkish culture, with its contributions (and Turks insist that they are many) to the making of Europe itself. Moreover, if Turkish culture was Byzantine in the West, it was Arabic in the East. Yet when western books acknowledge the indebtedness of Europe to Arab learning they rarely mention the fact that Arab learning flourished under a government which was Turkish. If it was the Turkish capture of Constantinople in 1453 which loosed the floodgates of Greek learning into western Europe, it was an enlightened Turkish rule which had enabled that culture, with the culture of the Arabs, to survive into modern times.

We westerners should make no mistake. The Turks claim that their government was enlightened, not the barbarian despotism which western books usually make it out to have been. The Ottoman Empire was always a conglomeration of races and religions; and both races and religions, if Turkish historians are right, received more toleration in medieval times than any racial or religious minority in Christendom. By the sixteenth century half the population of the Turkish Empire was Christian; but both before and after 1453 Christians of all sorts in Turkey had greater freedom than non-Catholics in western Europe: so great a freedom that many Christians were loyal servants of the Ottoman government, and many more decided to turn Turk. Persecutions of course there were—as bad as persecutions in western Europe, and no worse. If unbelievers were killed, at least they were not burnt

alive, and in fact there is good evidence that persecution was
rarely religious, almost always political—like the persecutions under our own Henry VIII and Elizabeth I, and unlike
those under our own Mary I.

By the end of the seventeenth century the Turkish flood
had spent its force. By the beginning of the eighteenth, Turkey
was already being represented as the Sick Man of Europe, and
during the nineteenth Europe was as worried by Turkish
weakness as she had previously been by Turkish strength. As
the European and African provinces fell away, it seemed as
though the Sick Man must die. Then came Ataturk, to complete the process which had only been arrested by long
decline, making Turkish culture at last European in character.

How far it is safe to accept all this Turkish case, western
historians have still to decide.

*   *   *

Clearly we need to re-examine our notions of what we
mean by the word 'Europe', and our notions of what Europe
in fact is: still more our notions of what it has been in the past.
For the Europe of history has always been changing its
identity. The very history of the name 'Europe' is worth
investigating. The Father of History himself was puzzled
about it. 'I have no idea,' says Herodotus, 'why we call the
world, which after all is one, by three different names, all
names of women [Europa, Asia, Africa]: nor why the frontiers
of Europe are said to be the Egyptian Nile and Colchian
Phasis—or, alternatively, according to some, the Maeotian
Tanais and the Crimean ferry. . . . The Persians consider as
theirs Asia and its barbarian inhabitants: Europe and the
Hellenic world they regard as a place apart.' This may have
seemed to Herodotus very parochial of the Persians; like most
later historians, he failed to realize the parochialism of his
own people, who 'regarded as a place apart' everywhere out-

side the Greek-speaking lands. The Greeks were unaware that in Hebrew and some other Semitic languages the word 'Europe' was cognate with 'Erebus'—the place of outer darkness where the chosen people did not dwell. To literary Greeks, Europeans were the descendants of the nereid Europa, and because Zeus fathered them in the guise of a white bull the Europeans were, unlike the normal majority of mankind, a sort of modified albino.

Outside the realm of legend the Greeks had no fixed notion of Europe. Some of them used the name for a part of Thrace, some for central Greece, some for the whole of Hellas and some eventually for Hellas and all the lands to the north—no one knew how far they stretched. In the days of Alexander the Great and the Roman Empire the very name of Europe became meaningless. *Cives Romani* abounded in Asia as in Europe in a way which made nonsense of both names. Roman geographers stuck to the word 'Europe', but Polybius and Strabo and Ptolemy all meant different things by it. With the Byzantine Empire, East Europe and West Asia became even more confounded; and although by that time Catholic Christianity had promised to make an entity of Christendom, the promise was never fulfilled. Catholicism and Orthodoxy split Christendom in two; at the Reformation Catholicism itself was splintered, and that ended any possibility of a united Europe built by the Church.

In any case, of the three elements which had made Europe what it is—Christian, Roman, Greek—Christianity at least was Asiatic. It began in Palestine, and its first offshoots were the Seven Churches of Asia, before it was brought to Europe by a Roman citizen of Tarsus in Asia Minor. And if in its beginnings one of the principal elements of Europe was Asian, in these days of the Council of Europe one member of the Council is not only Asian but Muslim. Thus in our own time, as in the days of the early Church, it is difficult to maintain that Christianity is an essential element in European culture.

What, then, are the criteria which make Europe what it is? We need to establish those criteria if we are to know what subjects in European history it is desirable to teach. It is time for another reassessment of history curricula throughout the schools of Europe. Often enough in the past we have had to jettison outworn practices—when we first abandoned drum and trumpet history; when we began to include imperial in political history; when we turned from a history wholly political to a history at least partly social; when, after the First World War, we made history for the first time international. We need now to take a step further—several steps. We have not only to find some means of including in our teaching the history of other nations and other races than our own; we have also to find new ideas about the sort of things which the history of any nation or race should contain. What are really the cultural factors which, because it is they which have made Europe European, must be taught to the future citizens of Europe? None of the really vital things which have managed to do that ought to be omitted. Some of them we teach already, and since they are vital they must not be pushed into the background merely because we wish to blaze new trails. Christianity, though it began in Syria and Asia Minor; Hellenism, though the earliest and greatest Greek poems were Asiatic; Romanism, though it eventually spread well east of the Mediterranean—these three are nevertheless such incontestable foundations of European culture that we might well teach more of them. Nor dare we say much less than we do now about the political and economic foundations of the West. There is the evolution of oligarchy into aristocracy, whether in the cities of Hellas, or on the plains of Germany from the time of Tacitus onwards, or throughout feudal Europe, or even in our own days when we have replaced feudal *magnati* by industrial magnates. There is the still more characteristically European evolution of democracy, Greek or parliamentary or socialist or Communist—all of them democracy with a difference, but all equally European. There is the exclusively European, or at least western, emergence of the nation-state in recent centuries, and its no less exclusively European corollary of colonialism and the white empires. There is even, for what it is worth in education, the evolution of war, from phalanx through feudal levy and bowman to its culmination as the universal destroyer. All these things we teach already, and the teaching of them has its real value for understanding the true character of Europe.

But just as we have hitherto neglected many lands not our own, so we have also neglected many subjects in history which it has simply not occurred to us to teach. We have been so preoccupied with politics and its social fringes that teachers have not thought of teaching (largely because historians have not thought of investigating) many other significant factors in the evolution of Europe. Only now are our leading historians beginning to urge us to take more notice of these things. Perhaps the most characteristically European of all social institutions is monogamy, and its corollary the one-generation family. Almost everywhere but in Europe and the lands which have been Europeanized a man may take more than one wife. Consequently, the European type of family is unique among mankind. How has this come about? Historians do not tell us, and teachers do not teach us. The normal European town and the normal European village are also unique, and this uniqueness extends to the larger units into which towns and villages are grouped—counties and departments and *Länder* and the rest. Here again we need to learn, and then to teach, how and why these things are so. In a quite different direction, there are the typical European characteristics of writing and literature. Where does our alphabet come from, and why do we write from left to right? Why have we alone evolved the novel, and why has it become preoccupied with an attitude towards sexual affection found only in Europeanized parts of the world? Why did our poetry tie itself so long to rhyme, and why did it not follow the Anglo-Saxons into alliteration or the Hebrews into the parallelisms of the Psalms? Why has blank verse flourished here and failed to flourish elsewhere in the world? These are only a few of the topics habitually neglected by European history teachers, though some appreciation of them all is essential if Europeans are to know what Europe is and how it developed.

Most significant of all, perhaps, is the European approach to philosophy. Europe is the home of logic—even of the syllogism, which has been fastened upon our minds by Plato and Aristotle and Euclid and the medieval schoolmen, and clamped down upon us by the philosophers of the Renaissance. Western philosophers—not the greatest, but most of the ordinary ones—constantly approach the problems of human thought as though accurate thinking were possible only in syllogisms. Yet all the commonest activities of our lives are directed by thought processes which are not syllogistic. We choose our food and our friends and our homes and our wives and our careers and nearly everything that matters by the light of a reason which is not deductive but intuitive. If we in the West are to realize the shortcomings of our own thinking, we shall have to learn and teach more about the uses of intuition in the East. This is particularly true in those advanced regions of thought which we call science. Our careful step-by-step thinking has enabled us to build a body of practical knowledge unrivalled in human history. Science (especially industrial science) is one of the greatest and most typical triumphs of the European genius, and the history of science ought to be taught in every European school. Beyond Europe, however, there have been other sorts of science, less precise perhaps, yet not less fruitful in the elucidation of truths. And whatever we in the West may think, the inhabitants of Hiroshima will hardly agree that eastern science has been less beneficial to humanity than the science of Europeans.

Some of this, no doubt, will seem at first sight far removed from teaching in schools. Yet why should it seem more strange for us to teach the history of the most vital things in our lives than the history of the less vital? Children come into contact with poetry far more than with politics, and if they can learn to approach poetry with a less national, even a less European, bias, they will acquire an appreciation of it which will serve them much better in adult life than a knowledge of merely political history. They will be far better off listening to broadcasts from the greatest poets than to broadcasts from the greatest politicians. Poetry deals with matter of much more moment for the human soul than politics, and if the subject-matter of history is (as the Historical Association claims) *quidquid agunt homines*, then our history teaching should say a good deal more about poetry and a good deal less about politics than it does at present.

It is the same with the other arts, and most of all perhaps with music—the art which, in our radio age, has the widest appeal of all. For every political broadcast which he hears the child of today hears thousands of tunes, to most of which he (like his elders) listens without discrimination. It is surely absurd for the historian of our day, claiming all human activity as his province, to act as though politics occupies more of our time than all the arts. It is surely ill-balanced of him to say more about Nikias than about Sophocles, more about Savonarola than about Michaelangelo, more about Carteret than about Hogarth: or to write, as every historian does, as though life in the nineteenth century had been more influenced by the ballot than by the piano. Certainly the ballot is characteristically European—but not more characteristically European than our tempered keyboard, or all the other

European limitations to music which tend to stand between Europeans and the music which is being written in our time. By all means let the history of music be taught in music lessons and not in history lessons. But at least, the history taught in schools could cease to imply that music and art have had less influence in Europe than the comings and goings of parliamentarians.

There are, in fact, no end of considerations urging us to regard our present attitude to history and to our history teaching as out of date. If only a few of these considerations are valid, they are enough to confirm the need for a complete and ruthless overhaul both of the history written in the academies and of the history taught in the schools of Europe. We need fewer historians determined to dive ever deeper into archives: more historians able and willing to take as their parish the whole world, and all that man does in it. Leading historians in Europe for the past half-century and more have been too fond of using X-rays rather than searchlights. Till they change their ways, European school teaching will have to continue doling out to its pupils a history that omits many of the most characteristic and significant achievements of their continent.

Fortunately, the historians have already begun to change their ways. A Regius Professor of history has told us that archivism has gone too far. The biggest one-man historical work produced in this century is based mainly not upon original research but upon other books; it takes as its subject every civilization which has ever existed on the face of the earth—and among them there is no civilization called 'European'. Another contemporary historian calls our European inheritance 'a thicket of dead-ends', and urges us to see 'a new view of the European past, adapted to the new perspectives in which the old Europe stands in a new age of global politics and global civilization'. In this he is only echoing

Theodore Roosevelt after an interval of half a century: 'the Mediterranean era died with the discovery of America. The Atlantic era is now at the height of its development, and must soon exhaust the resources at its command. The Pacific era, destined to be the greatest of all, is just at its dawn'. If this is true, ruthless revision of our history teaching needs to go far beyond the confines of Europe. Indeed, as we have seen, Europe has no confines; our global age knows neither geographical nor cultural frontiers. To the east of Europe, neither the Urals nor the Ural is any longer significant; the culture of Leningrad—even of London—has spread to Vladivostock. Westwards, the culture of Europe spread to New York, and has long been re-echoed from Hollywood. Modern children need preparing (and the history lesson has to do its share) for life in a world where the same films are seen and similar programmes heard all round the equator and from Pole to Pole. Sooner or later the history of our schools will have to be genuinely world history. In that history Europe has certainly played a key part, and in all history teaching Europe must always occupy a most prominent place. But the time has gone by when, in schools or anywhere else, nine-tenths of the history taught can safely be devoted to a quarter of the world's inhabitants.

6

Early History of a Movement[1]

WHENEVER there are wars, the peoples grow weary of war, and try to devise some means of abolishing it. In Europe, the sixteenth to eighteenth centuries were periods of protracted wars, which produced a spate of proposals for perpetuating peace: the *Grand Dessein* of Henry IV or Sully, the *Law of War and Peace* of Grotius, the *Code of International Law* drawn up by Leibnitz, Penn's *Essay towards the establishment of an European Diet*: the various projects for peace and international arbitration by St. Pierre and Rousseau and Bentham and Kant. Then, in the nineteenth century, 'Peace Congresses' met from 1843 onwards—some of them under the presidency of Victor Hugo, whose work against war was not confined to diatribes against Napoléon le Petit. In 1849 one of these congresses prescribed, as a remedy for 'those political prejudices and other hereditary hatreds which have so often been the cause of disastrous wars . . . the better education of youth, and other practical methods'. The 1867 congress even saw the establishment of a periodical called *The United States of Europe*. But this did not last long, and in 1893 there was a return to education as one of the main paths to peace, in a demand for 'such a revision

[1] The first part of this chapter owes much to an unpublished essay by A. C. F. Beales, Reader in Education in the University of London King's College.

of manuals of instruction as will eliminate false and misleading representations'.

Although this was perhaps the first international declaration against the dangers in textbooks, the idea had been in the air for some time. It is pleasant to record that the first attempt to do something practical about it was the work of an Englishman. In this same year (1893) was published *A History of England with the Wars Left Out*, by G. Pitt. The book was little used, and its author is almost forgotten, but it was a landmark in textbook revision, because it sounded the death-knell of the drum-and-trumpet histories in the country. They took an unconscionable time a-dying, but the 1914–18 war finished them off in all schools where history was taken seriously.

That, of course, was the war to end war. Almost as soon as it was over two major steps were taken towards the revision of history books. In the Scandinavian countries (Norway, Sweden, Denmark and Finland) 'Norden Associations' had already been established with a view to co-ordinating their cultural activities. Each of the countries has its own association, and one of their principal activities is examining one another's school books. This began as early as 1920, and in the next year the whole question of textbook bias was taken up in a big way. The Carnegie Foundation for International Peace set on foot an enquiry into the history textbooks of all the countries which had taken part in the war—fifty-three of them; in 1924 a vast two-volume report found them all guilty, in varying degrees, of national prejudice.

This provided the young League of Nations with useful ammunition. In 1926 the League's International Committee for Intellectual Co-operation took the greatest step forward ever known in textbook reform, under the lead of the Spanish delegate, Casares. His name is immortalized (at any rate in the history of international education) by the 'Casares Resolution', which proposed, and better still produced, the first broadly international machinery ever established for regular text-book revision. The machine was imperfect, and before the next war it ground to a standstill: but it was the first, and it deserves to be remembered. It invited every member of the League to set up a National Committee charged with the task of examining foreign history books and reporting instances of national bias to the home country of the book concerned.

The scheme was a good one, but it was executed badly. The National Committees consisted almost wholly of distinguished historians who (as it naturally seemed to them) had more important things to do than read school-books. To distinguished historians school-books seem dull, and sometimes stupid—though but for the dull and stupid history books of their youth they would not have become distinguished historians. At any rate, between the dullness and the stupidity, the distinguished historians rarely bothered to read them, and still more rarely bothered to make recommendations about them to the National Committees of other nations. Long before the Second World War broke out the Casares procedure had died of neglect. But it had not died in vain. When another world war was over the spirit of Casares haunted the educators of a new war-weary generation, and textbook reform got well under way much more rapidly than in the nineteen-twenties.

Besides, by 1945 textbook reformers had more than the Casares procedure to build upon. A report, published by the International Congress of Historical Science in 1930, on history teaching (elementary, secondary and university) in fifty-five countries, produced a wealth of evidence about harmful national preconceptions. Next year the republics of South America did what the United States had done in 1916 —examined their own books, and resolved that in future 'textbooks and programmes will not contain any expressions or judgments which reveal a feeling of hostility towards another country'. The wording of this resolution is significant. Although made by university teachers it was not afraid of going outside the realm of merely factual inaccuracies. These South American universities realized, as the universities of Europe have been slow to realize, that the real trouble is not factual inaccuracy, which is easily detected, but verbal nuances which, however accurate in fact, imply 'expressions or judgments which reveal a feeling'. It is much easier for a textbook or a teacher to reveal a feeling than to drive home a fact, accurate or inaccurate.

All this was promising: the right climate of opinion was forming, and in the same year the International Committee for Intellectual Co-operation could announce that 'a world movement is growing up for the reform of school textbooks by removing elements prejudicial to the mutual understanding of nations'. A few months earlier an International Federation of Teachers' Associations had been established at the Hague, though it came to nothing. But in the following year South America once more led the way—momentously, by putting the compulsory revision of textbooks into an international treaty between governments. The first to accede to this treaty were the four governments of Argentina, Brazil, Uruguay and Mexico, and in 1938 it was extended to include all the other states of South America. At the same time the Norden Associations of Scandinavia put their own scheme on a permanent basis by setting up a standing Joint Committee for History Teaching. This committee almost immediately established a new and vital precedent by beginning to exchange, not only printed books, but manuscripts before they even went to a publisher.

Meantime (in 1935) another bound forward had been taken. France was still France, and occupying the Saar;

Germany was still Germany, and under Nazi domination.
Yet in that year, at the suggestion of the Berlin Association
of History Teachers, French and German historians got together to thrash out their educational differences. The result
was a famous (even infamous) Memorandum, agreed by both
sides, setting forth points in the historical relations of their
two countries which all of them felt able to accept. This
could have provided an excellent programme for history
teaching and textbook writing in France and Germany, but it
was bedevilled from the start by circumstances both educational and political. The Nazi government denounced it, and
disavowed the German teachers who had helped to compile
it. This was no doubt to be expected. But, quite unexpectedly,
the Memorandum was also denounced very vigorously in
England, on the ground that it merely papered over cracks.
This was true: the cracks did in fact widen till the whole
building collapsed in 1939. Yet the papering over was at
least evidence that even in the nineteen-thirties there was
goodwill between the history teachers of the two most
inveterately hostile countries in Europe. This evidence stood
international education in good stead when the next war was
over.

In their intransigence over the Franco-German Resolutions
of 1935 the English universities, though sincere, were surely
mistaken. At about the same time, too, England was responsible for another check to the reform of the history books,
and this time it was due, not to any misunderstanding, but to
our insistence on a very important principle—a principle
which has long marked our Ministry of Education as one of
the most liberal and enlightened in the world. The League of
Nations invited all its member states to sign a declaration
that they would initiate textbook reform in their own
countries. Thirty-one states agreed; seven refused, and among
the seven were Nazi Germany, the United States and Britain.

The reason given by the U.S.A. was that education there was the concern, not of the Federal Government, but of each of the forty-eight states. The reason given by Britain was that in no circumstances would a British government interfere with the complete liberty of teachers and textbook writers. An English teacher or textbook writer can teach or write pretty well what he likes without any intervention from the government at all. Our liberty in this is greater than that of any other country in the world. Even today few foreigners can bring themselves to realize this; in the nineteen-thirties it seemed wholly incredible. All they saw was that Britain had aligned itself with the Nazis in rejecting a liberal proposal of the League of Nations.

Then came the war, which suspended open internationalism almost everywhere. Yet during the war years internationalists were not idle. The very exigencies of war happened to provide English history teachers with an unexpected opportunity. As Germany occupied more and more of Europe, democratic statesmen and administrators and historians from abroad crowded as refugees into Britain. Wartime London was a hive of eminent foreigners, among them many educators. The Historical Association eagerly seized the occasion. At that time the Chairman of its International Committee was Sir Henry Marten, of Eton, himself the writer of widely used textbooks: its Secretary was A. C. F. Beales, author of, among other things, a *History of Peace*. At the end of the war Marten was succeeded by G. T. Hankin. Under the lead of these three men the Historical Association arranged conferences with eminent foreign statesmen and educators living in Britain, and from their joint deliberations emerged a scheme for textbook revision which the Association adopted. Till the end of the war this scheme was pigeonholed. Then it was communicated to the United Nations Organization, which at that time had too much to do and

E

pigeon-holed it again. For the next four years it lay forgotten, and then it emerged in an unexpected quarter, to play an influential part in the post-war educational renaissance.

There had also been activity abroad during the war. No sooner was America involved than, as in 1916, she became keenly interested in the bias of textbooks. In 1942 the American Council of Education initiated a very wide study of educational materials all over Latin America—800 textbooks, seventy-five films, and even such less obviously dangerous things as pictures and songs. Then in 1944 a joint conference of American and Canadian history teachers tackled their own mutual difficulties. After three years they produced a valuable *Study of National History Textbooks used in the Schools of Canada and the United States* which, in the American manner, abounded in lists of facts and tabulated statistics.

By that time Germany, and Japan, had collapsed and were occupied by Allies committed to a total uprooting of everything undemocratic. Among other things, all the Nazi history books, which had done so much to build up Hitler and his system, were destroyed. What were history teachers to do during history lessons in the new republics of Eastern and Western Germany? The educational experts sent into Germany by the Allies rushed round Europe in a frenzied search for history-teaching materials. Blackboards, time-charts, wall-maps, pictures, films, were poured into this German educational vacuum—anything which might enable the teachers of Germany to teach a history which was not Nazi. For the next two years the lot of the German history teacher was thoroughly miserable. Above him were the Allied educational authorities, insisting that his teaching should be democratic, whatever that might mean—and it meant two different things in Berlin and Bonn. Around him were his own headmasters and inspectors, insisting that his teaching should be not only efficient, but German. And below him were his pupils, who no doubt made the most of the opportunities afforded by their teacher's embarrassment.

And then, amid all this dearth of materials, there appeared in the east a little cloud like a man's hand; and before long there fell a refreshing rain. What happened was this: the Allied authorities had overlooked the most valuable of all teaching instruments, the teacher himself. All you need for teaching, an English educator once said, is a boy, a book and a birch. The German history teachers had their boys and their birches: soon they had a few books, then more and more, provided not by Allied overseers, but by Germans, who understood German education better even than the horde of Allied administrators, many of whom came from goodness knows where. These administrators had been told by their govern-ments—and so had the numerous English teachers sent over in groups to show German teachers how they could educate young Germans to become good Englishmen—that there were no competent teachers left in Germany; that the Nazis had eliminated the democratic ones, and the Allies had eliminated the Nazis, so that only incompetent substitutes had survived this double purge. In this, the Allied authorities were mistaken. There were, in fact, plenty of admirable teachers left in the German schools—the same men and women, apart from normal wastage, who had been there all the time. Most of them, no doubt, had bowed the knee to the Nazi Baal, as they had previously bowed the knee to the Ashtaroth of Weimar. Now, after the Nazi débâcle, they were prepared to bow the knee to Britannia, or Columbia, or Marx, rather than lose their jobs and see their families starve. Though they had not resisted the Nazis, they were not Nazi at heart; though the older of them had not resisted Weimar, they were not democrats at heart: though all were now anxious to stand well with the Allies, they were still Germans, and they solved their own textbook problems by providing their own textbooks.

The story of their production makes one of the few romances of textbook reform. At that time Germany was short of everything—not only books, but paper and binding materials. Nevertheless a series of booklets on history and its teaching, not bound but clipped together, and printed on what was almost blotting paper begged from the waste of a local journal, began to be published in Brunswick. The books were written, not for school children, but for teachers and students in training colleges, to whom it was sought to show how history could be taught in the new way. *Contributions to History Teaching* they were called, and the earliest of them were as hard on the eye as the newspaper on whose semi-absorbent scrap they were printed. But they reached, first the students of the Training College in Brunswick, then students and teachers in an ever-widening area of Germany. Written by German scholars and passed by the Textbook Sections of the Allied Control Commissions for Germany, they provided German teachers with a history they dared teach in the confidence that it was blessed from above—and most German teachers knew from bitter experience, in a way British teachers can never conceive, that to teach a history not blessed by authority was to court loss of living if not loss of life. With something safe to teach, the German teachers taught—without all the paraphernalia of apparatus provided by conquerors who seemed not to know what teachers are for.

All this began in Brunswick because there was a 'Brunswick Group' of Germans (business and professional men as well as teachers) who had always been opposed to Nazism, and who were now anxious that German thought should be led into channels more democratic and international. So far as textbook reform was concerned, the chief of these men was

Georg Eckert, Professor of History at the Brunswick Train-ing College. It had been his idea to use the newspaper scraps, and he was the author of the first of the *Contributions to History Teaching* (it was, significantly, about the Peasants' Revolt of the 1520's), and then editor of the whole series. A man of immense enterprise and unbounded energy, he is always casting about for fresh methods of bringing German education into line with that of the western democracies. In 1949, he happened to learn of the English Historical Associa-tion's scheme for textbook reform which had been devised during the war and then pigeon-holed. At that time he was working with another embodiment of restless energy, T. J. Leonard of the British Textbook Section of the Control Commission. Leonard, too, believed deeply in the vast influence of textbooks on political life, national and inter-national—he used to say that if Foreign Offices would read foreign history textbooks they could save all the money they spend at present on agents' reports about public opinion abroad. When these two men heard of the Historical Associa-tion plan they pounced upon it. Next year the Historical Association chose and the Foreign Office sent to Brunswick a team of history teachers to co-operate with the Brunswick Group. Within a few months this was followed by the first of the textbook exchanges between England and Germany, and they have gone on ever since—at first under the Historical Association, then by a private group of teachers who carried on temporarily when the Historical Association fell out, and since 1954 as part of the activities of the United Kingdom National Commission for UNESCO.

This Anglo-German exchange gave Professor Eckert a jumping-off ground, and he jumped with a vengeance. During the next few years he contrived to start exchanges between Germany and nearly every other country in western Europe, and some in America, and some in Asia. He also established, in 1951, the Brunswick International Schoolbook Institute, devoted wholly to the research and collection of archives necessary for improving school-books on an international level. Another was established at Delhi in 1955, as part of the Indian Government's Five-Year Plan. India since independence has been called the land of the blue-print, and there could hardly be a better illustration of this than the Textbook Research Institute at Delhi, which in its first year or two of existence set about revising over a hundred Indian textbooks, and has pushed such things as the statistical measurement of textbook qualities farther than they have gone anywhere else, even in America.[1]

Even before the twentieth century dawned, India was already impatient of the English textbooks with which its schools and colleges were flooded. But such phenomena as the Delhi Institute are, in part at least, first fruits of UNESCO's major project for mutual understanding between East and West. This is a ten-year plan, and its full harvest will not be reaped for at least a decade. But it has meant that among the teachers of East and West like has met like, and it has meant also the encouragement of spontaneous schemes for textbook exchange across the Great Divide. Germany was the first to cross the line, with exchanges between the Brunswick Institute and India and Japan (as well as Poland and Jugoslavia) in the first years of its existence. But the ancient ties between India and Britain have drawn their teachers together also, so that school-books and teachers' views are already flowing between the Delhi Institute and the National Commission for UNESCO in London.

UNESCO is so clearly fitted for such activities as textbook reform that it was naturally one of the first in the field when the war was over. While the occupied countries were being injected with a history which was, after all, a part of Allied

[1] In 1957 a similar institute was begun in Osaka University.

propaganda, UNESCO arranged conference after conference of teachers from many nations. In these UNESCO conferences, frank speaking and mutual understanding were easier than in meetings arranged by even the most altruistic of Foreign Offices and Education Ministries. As a result UNESCO has been able to scatter all over the world a spate of literature on international education, and a good deal of it has managed to by-pass the waste-paper baskets of offices and studies and common-rooms. It is all a long-term policy, and progress sometimes seems deadly slow; but public opinion is gradually awakening to the value of what is being done about history book revision. Leading articles about it in *The Times* and *The Guardian* are evidence enough of that. And textbook reform is so obviously beginning to pay dividends that the example of UNESCO has been followed by such voluntary international bodies as Fraternité Mondiale and the Bureau de L'Enfance et de la Jeunesse, and by the less voluntary and less international Council of Europe.

There has been no difficulty in getting the school teachers, at any rate, to play their part. Between the wars someone described the English teaching profession as 'riddled with internationalism', and that was probably quite as true of the teachers of many countries abroad. Today, at least as regards textbook reform, it is truer abroad than in Britain. British teachers are all too ready to believe that because our textbook writers are the freest of all from official interference, our textbooks are therefore freest of all from national bias. That, unfortunately, is not true; but it has had the effect of holding back from international textbook reform many British teachers whose internationalism is beyond question. The lead has been taken by foreigners. In fact, since the end of the war, the movement has had the good fortune to be directed by a small group of men in various countries who are not only distinguished teachers, but also administrators of experience.

One of the most conspicuous is the Rektor of the Frogner School in Oslo, Haakon Vigander. He had long been taking part in the textbook exchanges of the Norden Associations; he was perhaps the first to point out that the danger in textbooks lies in those undefinable and elusive prejudices which lurk undetected in the mental make-up of all human beings, academic historians as well as school teachers. One result of this initital impetus was that the movement since 1945 has been mainly in the hands of school teachers and not of university historians, as it was between the wars; so that this time textbooks have been really read and really revised. Vigander, who gave this lead, has since remained one of the most active and respected workers in the whole movement. With him there have been from the beginning not only Professor Eckert of Brunswick, but Professor Bruley, history teacher at the Lycée Condorcet in Paris, and President of the Société des Professeurs d'Histoire et de Géographie, and André Puttemans, history inspector of the Belgian Ministry of Education. All of them have given freely of their counsel, based on a wide experience in the international aspects of education, and all of them have been responsible for valuable publications on textbook reform.

The movement has also been fortunate, since 1945, in the sympathetic co-operation of a number of university historians from all over Europe. Between the wars the interest of university historians was not sufficient to secure success for the Casares Plan. This time most of the hard work has been done by school teachers, but many university teachers have found themselves attracted, and their approval has been an invaluable guarantee that the claims of exact scholarship are not being overlooked. School teachers are rarely authorities on any one period of history. Their interests are general, and there is always a danger that the exigencies of good teaching may clash with the exigencies of academic objectivity. The co-operation of university historians, some of them of very high standing, has been a useful curb on teachers whose educational enthusiasm might otherwise have outrun their historical discretion.

* * *

And now, how is it all done? What are the measures actually taken for the removal of bias in history books, and to what extent are they succeeding? It is easier to talk than to act. Of conferences there is no end—especially of international conferences, which so often seem to let off steam and then get nothing done. This was the case with textbook reform between the wars, when the practical idealism of Casares promised so much, and interested so many influential people, but was almost wholly unsuccessful. Since 1945 things have been different. Conferences there have been in abundance, and they have let off steam. But this time there has been action in abundance too. Many hundreds (perhaps thousands) of history books have been examined and criticized, often during the course of the conferences themselves. A good many of the conferences have formed themselves into working parties, and have met in full session only to approve (or reject) what the working parties have done. The conferences have therefor often ended not merely in the production of recommendations for action later, but in completed reports which could be communicated at once to educational authorities or authors or publishers, or whoever they were intended to reach. This has been the practice in all the six conferences held by the Council of Europe, and in a number of others besides.

One reason for this contrast between successful achievement now and comparative failure under the League of Nations is that UNESCO has avoided one serious defect in the Casares Plan. Instead of presenting the history teachers of the world with a cut-and-dried scheme ready-made and

E*

sent down from above, UNESCO first watched the teachers making their own experiments. Soon after the war, notably in conferences at Brussels and Sèvres, UNESCO brought out into the open the need for textbook reform; but as soon as it saw Germans and French and Belgians and English, as well as various kinds of Americans, starting to exchange books, it let them alone. The Casares Plan was a scheme which would have worked but never found the people to work it. This time UNESCO propounded no scheme; instead, it allowed despairing teachers and textbook writers to get together and hack their way through the textbooks. Of course mistakes were made: people were offended in all directions—archivists who believe that facts are the only form of truth; professional philosophers of history who distrust the amateur philosophizing of pedagogues; nationalists believing more or less in 'my country right or wrong'; internationalists and other ideologists with an avowed or hidden axe to grind; holders of group prejudices everywhere; and of course all those who believe it dangerous to embark upon any task without a scheme so well-laid that it could not possible gang agley. To all these the notion of school teachers tinkering with school history seemed abhorrent. All of them preferred the devil they knew to the devil which these interfering school teachers might raise.

The school teachers themselves, however, were so weary of the devil they knew that they resolved to exorcize him at all costs, and to get on with the job without waiting for an infallible formula of exorcism. So they took a dozen German books here and a dozen French or British or Belgian or American books there, and pointed out specific passages or general opinions which were likely to arouse international misunderstanding or even hatred. No water-tight scheme; precious little philosophy; merely bundles of books confronting bunches of teachers, each of whom, having read his book,

'struck his finger on the place
And said, Thou ailest here, and here.'

Some of the criticisms were just, some were unjust; some
relevant, some irrelevant. But at least the books were being
overhauled, and that alone created a climate of opinion for
the movement to grow in.

Then, when things were clearly getting done, UNESCO
offered to help—not to direct the schemes, still less to absorb
them; merely to help—with advice, with the promotion of
liaisons, with the defrayment of some of the expenses when
these were a difficulty. The highly organized enterprises of
the International Schoolbook Institute at Brunswick; the
vague gropings of a group of English teachers with no official
backing from anywhere; and between these two extremes
many other very diverse forms of activity—all were and are
encouraged by UNESCO to go their own way, but to go it
together, serving the general cause each in its own particular
fashion.

It is all the more surprising that Britain has been backward
in this business, since the method adopted has been what we
so much like to call typically British—muddling through and
all the rest of it. Perhaps we feel that foreign muddling makes
a muddle. That, at any rate, was how textbook reform was
begun this time. It was not until after some years of practical
experiment that a pattern of operation emerged, and the
efforts being made could be classified. Even now the classifica-
tion is hardly more than tentative, but at least it can be said
that every scheme is of one of three kinds—unilateral, bi-
lateral, or multi-lateral. Unilateral reports are the work of one
country alone, like the American report on the treatment of
Asia in American textbooks; or *History Without Bias?*, the
report on English history books by the English Council of
Christians and Jews. No doubt the co-operation of the five

Norden groups in Scandinavia should be classed as multi-lateral, but the most ambitious of multi-lateral projects has been that of UNESCO with regard to the relations of East and West, in which every member of the United Nations has been asked to report on its own textbooks, and the reports are co-ordinated by a multi-national committee, for publication by UNESCO itself.

Most schemes, however, are bi-lateral exchanges between couples of nations. Even the Brunswick Institute works in this way, with its radiation of separate schemes to dozens of nations around the globe. As early as 1944 the United States and Canada conducted a bi-lateral investigation and issued a joint report, and this is the pattern which has been most commonly followed. It is worth while remembering that one of the earliest bi-lateral investigations was between countries which have been inveterate enemies for at least a century—France and Germany. That this was so successful, against all odds, is no doubt due as much as anything to the sympathy and forbearance, as well as the scholarship, of the Frenchman and the German who took the initiative in their respective countries.

None of the schemes are without their pitfalls, and we in Britain have had our share of these. Unlike most other countries, we have no national association of history teachers. There are history committees of the American Councils on Education and the Social Studies: there is the Société des Professeurs d'Histoire et de Géographie: there is the history section of Arbeitsgemeinschaft Deutscher Lehrerverbänder. But the English Historical Association refuses to regard itself as a teachers' association, and in fact half of its members are non-teachers. There is no body which can claim to represent the history teachers of Britain, and for a long time foreign associations were at a loss whom to approach here. A solution was at last found when responsibility for all the British textbook exchanges was assumed by the U.K. National Commission of UNESCO, but this is not without its disadvantages. It might even be regarded as the betrayal of a fundamental principle of the Ministry of Education, with which the National Commission is linked, however unofficially, whereas the Ministry supposes itself to have nothing to do with the contents of textbooks. Still, this is not the first time in British history that a British institution has glanced aside from its principles in order to solve a practical problem.

At any rate, history textbooks are now flowing freely all over the world, and criticisms are flowing as freely in the opposite directions. Yet so far, all is talk. What has been done? What practical consequences have followed all the conferences and criticisms? What difference has it all made to the textbooks—and the teaching and the taught?

The easiest way of answering these questions (and probably the least satisfactory) is to count the number of changes which have been made in printed pages. If a German *Gutachten* has complained of some *Histoire Française* that it has misrepresented the amount of German spoken in Alsace, what alterations have since been made in the *Histoire Française*? Have its later editions given the correct percentage of German-speakers in Alsace? Or if an Indian criticism has complained that some *English History* gives only Indian atrocities in its account of the Mutiny, has a later edition of the *English History* either added the British atrocities or deleted the Indian ones? This line of approach has been much followed in such extremities of East and West as India and America, in both of which statistics are perhaps over-popular. Some of the American reports even go so far as to count the number of words or lines or pages which have been altered in this book or that as a result of foreign criticism, to reduce these figures to percentages, and so to offer a mathematical measurement of the effectiveness of textbook reform.

Methods of that kind appeal to few teachers in Britain—or for that matter in Germany or France or Italy or Belgium. In fact, such statistical tables when applied to textbook reform have most of the disadvantages and few of the advantages of all statistical appraisement. A *Histoire Française* may be most meticulous about its proportions of German-speaking Alsatians, but if thereby it gives the reader a general impression that because most Alsatians speak German therefore Alsace is more German than French, it will be wrong. Alsace is French, not by reason of any mathematical proportion of any sort, but because the nebulous elements of French culture have permeated the Alsatian people for several centuries. No doubt the cumulative effect of factual misrepresentations can be very harmful, and it is certainly desirable to suppress them. But the success or failure of textbook reform cannot be measured by the removal from existing books of errors in details. Making changes in printed books is not such a simple matter as some people think. The printed word may be a mighty means of enlightenment, but it is also a powerful obstacle to change. Most textbook writers write their books in an honest attempt to help teaching in some new way. But their publishers, in publishing the books, must make money, and it reduces their dividends if they consent to a frequent or drastic alteration of the pages which they have paid to have printed. Some publishers are kind, and allow as much alteration as they can afford: but all are human, and not many textbook writers like badgering their publishers for changes which seem anything less than imperative. A number of books in a number of countries have in fact made alterations in detail—some quite considerable; and in all cases the criticisms have been sent on to author or publisher or both. But it is too much to expect any publisher, working on narrow margins of profit, to scrap whole pages every time foreign criticisms come in. And nothing less than whole pages will suffice, since the complaints are less frequently about matters of detail than about nuances of phraseology affecting perhaps not merely pages, but the whole book. In Britain we suffer more from this state of things than most other countries. With us, if we want a textbook changed, we must ask an author to give up time and a publisher to give up money. More blessed in this respect is the country where textbooks are the business of the government, which can alter them as often as it pleases, out of the tax-payer's pocket.

For such reasons, tangible and intangible, textbooks will never be corrected as much as they should. A far better criterion of the efficiency of textbook exchanges is their influence, not on the books criticized, but on books published after the criticisms have been made. So much has been said already, and is being said repeatedly, about what is wrong in the existing books, that teachers everywhere are becoming alive to the dangers lurking in all textbooks. Consequently, the teachers are handling with greater caution the books they are using already; and authors of new books, more aware of the pitfalls than formerly, are more alert to avoid them. The process works slowly, but new books are already profiting, and they will profit more and more, from the criticism of old books. The new books are, in fact, better than the old ones; but the new books themselves are being criticized in their turn, so that the whole process is cumulative, and its full effects will not be seen for a generation or more of textbook writing. Besides, the Norden plan of submitting books for criticism while they are still in manuscript is being copied outside the Norden countries; and at least one author has taken the trouble to send to various countries abroad those parts of his manuscript which deal with the history of the countries concerned.

All this, and more which easily escapes notice, is evidence that the right climate of opinion is being formed in various parts of the world—and that is a more valuable result than any amount of detailed correction of existing errors. We must not lose sight of the end in the means. Our ultimate aim is not, as is often supposed, the correction of mistakes in school-books, or even the publication of better school-books than before. The ultimate aim is not even to eliminate bias from the history teaching of either schools or universities. All these are directed at the improvement of school teaching, whereas our ultimate target is not so much children at school, as the adults which those children are to become. When we correct a school-book, we sow seeds which may bear fruit after a generation. But when we secure publicity for such correction, we contribute to this year's harvest. There is great value, not merely in getting group prejudices removed from the school-books, but in persuading public opinion in general, at this present moment, that corrections are needed in the school-books; that group prejudices are rampant everywhere today, largely due to the school-books of yesterday; and that if they are not now abandoned they will pass on to the school-books of tomorrow. This education of adult public opinion is done far better when textbook criticisms are publicized than by the criticisms themselves. When the Council of Christians and Jews published its report on bias in English books, *The Times* had a leader about it. The Report itself reached perhaps thousands of readers, mostly teachers and other educators, who might modify some of their teaching accordingly. But *The Times* leader reached millions of readers and spread a knowledge of textbook revision and group prejudice more widely on that one day than any educational report could achieve in years.

Still, the reading of daily papers is not only daily but ephemeral, and although a *Times* leader reaches the educated opinion of the world on one day, there is need for a much more repetitive impact upon the educators themselves. This is being achieved by articles which appear pretty regularly in the educational periodicals everywhere. In Britain, perhaps less than a dozen educational periodicals have interested themselves and their readers in textbook reform. In France and in Belgium, where the man in the street likes to be 'intellectual', textbook reform has at times been 'news' in the journalistic sense. In the United States, many more journals of many more kinds have printed articles about it. And in Germany, with the Brunswick Institute behind it, news and views about textbook reform are disseminated, not only by the Institute's own *Year Book of History Teaching*, and by booklets (sometimes amounting almost to books) giving details of each bi-lateral exchange, but by articles, illustrated and otherwise, all over the semi-popular Press.

In fact, the early history of the movement is drawing to a close. Satisfactory methods of textbook exchange have been devised, and are widely in operation. Professional and public opinion has been aroused. The time has come for consolidation, and the problem is to decide in what directions consolidation shall take place. As far as Britain is concerned, shall we throw ourselves more heartily into the movement, or shall we continue the insular caution which has hitherto held us more aloof than most of the peoples of Europe and America? And by what means shall the fight against group prejudices be continued abroad?

It may be that the future lies with institutes like those already established at Brunswick, Delhi and Osaka. If so, money will have to be spent, and much of it must come from public funds, as it does there. Cost apart, however, there are countries (Britain is one of them) where anything so cut-and-dried tends to be unpopular. Here in Britain we have already tried various methods—exchanges with Germany under the aegis of the Foreign Office, of the Historical Association, and of the U.K. National Commission for UNESCO; exchanges with Germany and Denmark by a private group of teachers without any official support whatever; and the uni-lateral report on English books published by the Council of Christians and Jews, with financial backing from the Halley-Stewart Trust. All these methods have been successful in their varying degrees, and no doubt they are more congenial to British educators than a formal institute would be. Yet there are plenty of Education Institutes already in Britain, departments of British universities. It is rather remarkable that so far not one of these has lent a hand, though individual members of their staffs have been very helpful indeed. Nor has there been any formal co-operation from any of the teachers' own associations—the N.U.T., the Associations of Assistant Masters and Mistresses, and the rest, whereas the French Société des Professeurs d'Histoire et de Géographie, the Féderation Belge des Professeurs d'Histoire, the German United Teachers' Association, the Danish Union of History Teachers, and so on, have all played a very prominent part. In 1957 there was even established (mainly on Belgian initiative) an International Federation of History Teachers, which might perhaps prove a landmark in international education—but to whom in Britain should it apply to appoint the British delegate? Or shall the work, on an international scale, be left to such voluntary associations as the Carnegie Foundation, or Fraternité Mondiale, or the Bureau de la Jeunesse et de l'Enfance, all of which have already interested themselves deeply? Bodies like these usually know where to obtain funds —but usually, too, they have an axe of their own to grind.

Thus there are plenty of ways of tackling the problem, and the way chosen will no doubt differ from country to country in accordance with varying national predilections. Even if all the work all over the world is to be co-ordinated by UNESCO, the schemes co-ordinated may well vary greatly among themselves. There will be countries where organization is at a premium, like Germany and India, both already committed to Textbook Institutes; or like France, where organization may be loose but where thinking is precise; or like the United States, where rich men and rich institutions like doing things on the grand scale; or like Britain, where we enjoy seeming to do nothing at all, and yet manage, somehow, to get things done.

Whatever the methods adopted, there are dangers to guard against. But they must be faced, not used as an excuse for doing nothing. Certainly, internationalists seem to include an unusual number of cranks, who will have to toe the line. Certainly, attempts to be fair to foreigners can involve a tendency to be unfair to one's own country. Agreements may fail because they merely paper over cracks, hiding the fundamental fissions beneath; or they may succeed in rubber-stamping a false uniformity where free thought is essential. Critics are no less biassed than authors: criticisms are as liable as books to subjective prejudices. Activity in textbook reform, like many other admirable activities, may be used for propaganda and the building-up of prestige. All these things are true, and they cry out for caution. But though useful as traffic signs, they need not become road blocks. The way to deal with a dangerous bend is not to stop dead, but to proceed with care.

Moreover, even if we would stop, we cannot. The movement for reform is gathering momentum, and already it has spread to other subjects besides history. The Japanese are not the only oriental people to claim that the picture of eastern life presented in the average European geography book is a grotesque travesty of the truth; and similar complaints, less vociferous perhaps but no less insistent, are being heard in the West. Consequently, geography has already been included in some of the schemes for textbook exchange and criticism which have hitherto been confined to history. More recently, misgiving has spread to the teaching of languages and literatures. Language teachers are said to be so pre-occupied with matters of grammar and style that textbooks are chosen with far too little attention to their subject-matter. Books read mainly for their literary value, or because they are easy to translate, can implant very peculiar ideas of foreign life and culture in the open minds of the pupils who use them. In this, as earlier in history, Germany has led the way; the Research Institute of the German Society for Foreign Politics has taken up the whole question of what they call *Das Bild vom Ausland*—the impressions about foreign peoples received by German children at school; and joint investigations into bias in language teaching have been begun between German, French and English teachers and publishers.

Thus, if there are risks in going ahead, there are more risks in remaining as we are. History books and history teaching, and indeed all education, are at present vitiated by prejudices of many different kinds. They will continue to be so vitiated unless the prejudices are removed, not merely now, but constantly; for textbook reform cannot come to an end so long as textbooks continue to be used. Between the wars it was killed by indifference. Since the last war, it has made a good restart; it must not this time be killed by timidity. We are not taking a leap into the dark. The possible dangers are known well enough, but so are the inevitable gains. This is a retreat from what is realized to be bad, and a resolve, despite the risks, to advance towards something better.

Chief Authorities

During a lifetime of reading history books I have usually found footnote references to authorities more irritating than helpful, and I have therefore avoided them in this book. But as there may be readers who wish to pursue the subject at the level of research, I give below a list of the chief authorities I have used. It should, however, be realized that much of my information has been gleaned in private conversation or correspondence, or during the unrecorded activities of conferences; and for this, of course, it is impossible to give references.

I. UNPUBLISHED MATERIAL

(a) *Issued by UNESCO:*
Documents relating to the improvement of textbooks and teaching materials.
Summaries:

> *Some Reports of Bilateral Consultations on History Texbooks* (ED/CIM/2; Dec. 1954).
>
> *Learning About Other Cultures: Notes on Two Studies of Textbooks* (ED/CIM/1; Dec. 1954).
>
> Sidhanta, R.: *A Study of Basic Concepts relating to India* (ED/-CIM/6; May 1955).
>
> *The Brussels Seminar* (WS/O61.32; July 1951).
>
> *National Reports on the Treatment of Asia in Western Textbooks and Teaching* (ED/CIM/8–25, 1955).
>
> Extract from *L'Asie dans les Manuels belges* (ED/CIM/7; 1956).
>
> *Memorandum on a proposed Major Project to promote 'Mutual Appreciation of Asian and Western Cultural Values'* (UNESCO General Conference, New Delhi, 1956).
>
> *Committe of Experts on* the Treatment of Asian Cultures in *Western Textbooks and Teaching Materials: Agenda and Memorandum* (ED/CIM/Conf. 1 and 3; 1957).

(b) *Other unpublished material:*

Beales, A. C. F.: *Memorandum on Nationalism in the Teaching of History* (1939). *Draft Procedure for setting up an International Advisory Committee of Historical Experts for the Revision of National Bias in History Class Books used in Schools* (Adopted by the International Committee of the Historical Association 25th March 1944).

Lindsay, M.: *Notes on Educational Problems in Communist China* (New York: Institute of Pacific Relations, 1950, mimeographed).

Decisions Concerning the Reform of the Educational System (Administration Council of the Central People's Government, China, 1st Jan. 1951).

Council of Europe Reports of Conferences on The European Idea in the Teaching of History, 1953–58.

Report on the Indian-German Conference at the Internationales Schulbuchinstitut, Brunswick, Oct. 1954.

Wilson, Howard E.: *The Improvement of History Textbooks: A Plan for Action* (Report of address to the Brussels Conference of Fraternité Mondiale, 1955).

Notes Prepared by the Minister of Education, Kuala Lumpur, for the guidance of Heads of Schools and Publishers (Aug.–Sept. 1955).

Die Deutsch-französischen Beziehungen im Mittelalter: Ergebnisse der Deutsch-französischen Historiker-Tagung (Bamberg, 19th–22nd July 1956: Text mainly in French).

Ayerst, D.: *History Teaching in some Foreign Lands* (London, Ministry of Education; n.d.).

Parry, J.: *The Teaching of History in the Americas* (n.d.).

II.   OFFICIAL SYLLABUSES AND DIRECTIVES
(Some of these are not published)

Reglement for realskoleeksamen (Norway, Kirke-og-undervisnings-departementet, Oslo 1953).

Programmi di Insegnamento della Storia nelle Scuole Medie Inferiori e nel Ginnasio-Liceo Classico primo dell'anno 1940 (Italian Ministry of Public Instruction, n.d.).

Programmi, No. 2100 (Rome, Ministry of Public Instruction, n.d. since 1950).

Lehrpläne für die Grund-und-Oberschulen in der Sovjetischen Besatzungszone Deutschlands. Geschichte: 1. *Auflage* (Juli 1946);

2. *Auflage* (Sept. 1947). (Deutsche Verwaltung für Volks-bildung etc.)

Course of Study in World History (Philippines Bureau of Public Schools, Manila 1949).

L'Enseignement de l'histoire (Belgian Ministry of Education, Brussels 1952).

Instructions provisoires concernant la réforme de l'enseignement moyen (Brussels 1942).

Bekendtgørelse om undervisningen i gymnasiet (Danish Ministry of Education 1953).

Anordning angaende undervisningen i gymnasiet om fordringerne ved og eksamenopgivelserne til studenteksamen (*ibid.*) 1953).

Grundsätze zum Geschichtsunterricht (Empfehlung der Kultus-Minis-ter-Konferenz vom 17 Dezember 1953 in Bonn).

Geschichte in Wissenschaft und Unterricht (Bonn, Kultusminis-terium 1953 and 1954).

Enseignement de l'histoire (French Ministry of Education: Bulletin officiel de l'éducation nationale, 16th Dec. 1954).

Horaires et Programmes, enseignement sécondaire et supérieure (Grand Duchy of Luxemburg, Ministry of National Education, 1955–6).

Programme d'histoire pour l'enseignement primaire (Damascus: Syrian Ministry of Public Instruction, n.d.).

Programme d'histoire pour l'enseignement préparatoire (Iraq Ministry of Public Instruction, n.d.).

Revised Syllabus, Bombay State Education Department (n.d.).

Oideachas naisiunta/Notes for Teachers: History (Department of Education, Eire, n.d.).

L'utilisation du document dans l'enseignement de l'histoire (Paris, Centre national de documentation pédagogique: n.d.).

Official Syllabus for School Instruction. French West Africa (n.d.)

III. PUBLISHED BY OR FOR UNESCO

Vigander, H.: *Mutual Revision of History Textbooks in Nordic Countries* (1950).

Better History Textbooks (1950).

McLaurin, J.: *International Agencies: A Project Handbook for Authors and Publishers of Schoolbooks* (Ed/77: July 1950).

Febvre, L., and Crouzet, F.: *International Origins of a National Culture; Experimental Materials for a History of France* (ED/-TB/10, April 1951).

Hill, C. P.: *Suggestions on the Teaching of History* (1951).

Lauwerys, J. A.: *History Textbooks and International Understanding* (1951).

Recommandations pour l'enseignement de l'histoire (Paris: French National Commission for UNESCO, 1951).

L'enseignement de l'histoire et la compréhension internationale (ibid.)

Handbuch für die Neugestaltung von Schulbüchern und Lehrmittel (1951).

Strong, G. F.: *Teaching for International Understanding* (a statement prepared for the U.K. National Commission for UNESCO, 1952).

Lévi-Strauss, Claude: *Race and History* (1952).

Pour l'amélioration des manuels et de l'enseignement de l'histoire (Paris 1952).

The Contribution of Textbooks and Teaching Materials as Aids to the Development of International Understanding (Swiss National Commission for UNESCO, ED/116, Nov. 1952).

New Zealand School Textbooks and International Understanding (New Zealand National Commission for UNESCO, ED/118, Nov. 1952).

A Study of History and Geography School Textbooks (Norwegian National Commission for UNESCO, ED/117, Nov. 1952).

History, Geography and Social Studies: a summary of school programmes in 53 countries (1953).

Humanism and Education in East and West (1953).

Educational Studies and Documents, IV: *Bilateral Consultations for the Improvement of History Textbooks* (July 1953); X: *Education Abstracts* (Dec. 1953).

Education Abstracts: The Teaching of History (April 1955).

Ghisalberti, A. M.: *I convegni italo-francesi per la revisione dei manueli di storia* (Rome: Italian National Commission for UNESCO, 1954).

Documents relating to the Improvement of Textbooks and Teaching Materials (ED/143, May 1955).

The Treatment of Asia in Western Textbooks and Teaching Materials (ED/147, Nov. 1956).

Programmes et Manuels d'histoire: Suggestions en vue de leur amélioration (Swiss National Commission for UNESCO, April 1957).

McClure, D.: *The Treatment of International Agencies in School*

History Textbooks in the United States (U.S.A. National Commission for UNESCO, Washington, D.C., n.d.).
The Treatment of the West in Textbooks and Teaching Materials of South and East Asia (1958).

IV. PUBLISHED BY OR FOR THE INTERNATIONALES SCHULBUCHINSTITUT, BRUNSWICK

Internationales Jahrbuch für Geschichtsunterricht, 1951 ff.
Geschichtsunterricht in unserer Zeit: Grundfragen und Methoden (1951).
Zur Geschichte und Problematik der dänisch-deutschen Beziehungen (1952–3).
Deutschland und Frankreich im Spiegel ihrer Schulbücher (1954).
Geschichtsunterricht, Brücke zwischen den Völkern (1954).
Deutsch-Italienische Thesen über die geschichtlichen Beziehungen der beiden Völker im *19/20 Jahrundert* (partly in Italian; 1954).
Wie Andere uns sehen: die letzten 100 Jahre deutscher Geschichte in Europäischen Schulbüchern (1955).
Deutschen-Belgien, 1830–1945 (partly in French; 1955).
Kobata, A.: *Geschichte Japans* (1955).
Deutschland und England 1904–1914: *Empfehlungen der englisch-deutschen Historikertagung* 1955 (partly in English; 1955).
Schüddekopf, O.–E.: *Die internationale Schulbucharbeit: eine Bibliographie* (1956).
Deutschland und die Vereinigten Staaten (partly in English; 1956).
Meyer, E.: *Uber die Darstellung der deutsch-polnischen Beziehungen im Geschichtsunterricht* (1956).
Indien-Deutschland: Empfehlungen der indisch-deutschen Historiker-konferenz, Braunschweig 1954 (1956).
Deutschland und England 1918–33 (partly in English; 1957).
Banerji, J. K.: *Laying the Foundation of 'One World'* (1957).
Geschichtsunterricht in einer sich-wandelnden Welt (n.d.).

V. PUBLISHED BY THE HISTORICAL ASSOCIATION, LONDON

Reid, R. R., and Toyne, S. M.: *The Planning of a History Syllabus for Schools* (Pamphlet No. 128, 1944).
Teaching of History Leaflets, Nos. 2, 3, 4, 5, 6, 14, 15, 16 (various dates).

Common Errors in History (1945).
More Common Errors in History (1947).
Common Errors in Scottish History (1956).
Catalogue of an Exhibition of School History Books from 37 countries (Dec. 1952).
Hunt, J. W.: *British History Through Foreign Eyes* (1954).
Burston, W. H.: *Soviet History Teaching* (in *History*, Feb./June 1954).
History and Secondary Education in Scotland (1957).

VI. PUBLISHED BY THE SOCIETY FOR CULTURAL RELATIONS WITH THE U.S.S.R.

Gittis, I. V.: *Assessing the Pupil's Knowledge of History* (*Soviet Education No. 2*, 1945).
Hill, C.: *The Teaching of British History in the U.S.S.R.* (*Anglo-Soviet Journal*, Autumn 1951).
Two Secondary School Syllabuses (*Education Bulletin* No. 15, April 1953).
Secondary School Syllabus of Modern History (*ibid.* No. 17, Sept. 1953).
Averanoff, A. P., and Orloff, V. A.: *The English Revolution of the 17th Century. Methods of Treatment in Teaching* (Bulletin, History and Archaeological Section, May, August and Nov. 1954).
Revisions in History Teaching in Soviet Schools, 1956 (Information Bulletin, Vol. 3, No. 2, Nov. 1956).
Voprosy Istorii (Information Bulletin Vol. 4. No. 2, July 1957).
Aviation History (*ibid.*).
Conference of Orientalists (*ibid.*).

VII. MISCELLANEOUS

Batten, T. R.: *Handbook on the Teaching of Elementary School History and Geography in Nigeria* (Lagos 1933).
Alnor, K.: *Die nationalsozialistische Erziehungsidee im Schulunterricht* (Ziefeldt, Verlag Osterwieck/Harz, 1935).
Beale, H. K.: *Are American Teachers Free?* (in *Investigation of Social Studies in Schools*, New York, Scribner 1936).
Solis-Cohen, R. T.: *A Comparative Study of the History Program*

in English and American Secondary Schools (University of Pennsylvania, 1938).

Klagges, D.: *Geschichte als nationalpolitische Erziehung* (Verlag M. Diesterweg, Frankfort a/M. 1942).

American History in Schools and Colleges (New York, the Macmillan Co., for the American Historical Association etc. 1944).

Thursfield, R.: *The Study and Teaching of American History* (National Council for the Social Studies, Washington, D.C., 1946).

Vigander, H.: *The Teaching of History and International Understanding* (Report of the Hundorp Conference, 1946).

A Study of National History Textbooks used in the Schools of Canada and the United States (Washington, D.C., The American Council on Education, 1947).

The Foundations of Our Civilisation: Fundamental Postulates of Christianity and Judaism in relation to Human Order (London: Council of Christians and Jews, 1947).

Ramirez, R. (ed.): *La Enseñanza de la Historia en Mexico* (Mexico, Instituto Panamericano de Geografiá e Historia, 1948).

Bulletin 1347 (University of New York, 1948).

Deutsche-englische Geschichtslehrertagung, Braunschweig, 1–8 Juli 1949.

The Second Anglo-German Conference of History Teachers, Brunswick, July 1950 (in *History*, Vol. xxxv, p. 125, Oct. 1950).

Report of the Second Anglo-German History Teachers Conference at Brunswick, July 1950.

Report of the Third Anglo-German History Teachers Conference at Brunswick, July 1951.

Blount, C. H. C.: *The International Exchange and Review of History Textbooks* (in the *Cambridge Journal*, Vol. v., No. 2, 1951).

Results of School Examinations in Modern History (Soviet Studies II 4, April 1951).

Schnell, H.: *Der Geschichtsunterricht in Osterreich* (Internationales Jahrbuch für Geschichtsunterricht 1951).

Mielke, K.: *Der Geschichtsunterricht in den höheren Schulen* (in Geschichtsunterricht in unserer Zeit, Brunswick 1951).

Bing, H. F.: *The Study and Teaching of History in post-war Germany (History*, No. 126–7, Feb./June 1951).

Musgrove, F.: *History Teaching in African Secondary Schools* (in *Oversea Education*, Oct. 1951).

Bulletin de la Société des Professeurs d'Histoire et de Géographie: les entretiens franco-allemands (Mar./Oct. 1951).

History Textbooks (*Manchester Guardian*, 10 Dec. 1951).

Bining, A. C. and D. H.: *Teaching the Social Studies in Secondary Schools* (New York, McGraw-Hill, 1952).

The Teaching of History (Cambridge University Press, for the I.A.A.M., 1952).

Lousse, Emile: *Desseins, Limites et Perspectives: Les Stages de l'UNESCO, l'enseignement de l'histoire et l'orientation de la recherche* (Paris, Institut de l'Avenir, 1952).

Liu Shih: *China's New Educational System* (in *School and Society*, 29 March 1952).

Report by the Ministry of Education of the Central People's Government, China, concerning the Plan of Reorganisation for the Technical Colleges throughout the Country (*People's Daily* 16 April 1952).

Zinoviev, M. A.: *Soviet Methods of Teaching History:* translated from the Russian (American Council of Learned Studies, 1952).

Utechin, S. V.: *Secondary School Textbooks on History* (*Soviet Studies* IV, July 1952).

History in Soviet Schools (*Times Educational Supplement*, 22 Feb. 1952).

Fischer-Galati, S. A.: *The Teaching of History in the Schools of Rumania* (in *School and Society*. 15 Nov. 1952).

Rencontre pédagogique de professeurs d'histoire des pays Bénélux, Luxembourg, 9–11 Avril 1953: Rapport (Fraternité Mondiale).

Recommandations aux auteurs et éditeurs de manuels d'histoire sur l'histoire de Norvège (Bulletin de la Féderation belge des Professeurs d'histoire, 1953).

Eckert, G. (ed.): *Deutschland-Frankreich-Europa* (*Die Deutsch-französische Verständigung und der Geschichtsunterricht*) (Baden, Verlag für Kunst und Wissenschaft, 1953: see *Rencontres franco-allemands* below).

Portal, R.: *L'Enseignement de l'Histoire en Czechoslovakie* (*Information Historique*, Mars/Avril 1950, summarized in Documentation française, 17 Nov. 1953).

L'Enseignement de l'histoire en France et dans quelques pays étrangers (Paris, *Notes et études documentaires* No. 1805, 1953).

Ramirez, R.: *La Educación en Mexico y la enseñanza de la historia en las escuelas del pais* (in *Internationales Jahrbuch für Geschichtsunterricht*, II, 1953).

Puttemans, A.: *La réforme de l'enseignement de l'histoire en Belgique* (Geneva, *Fraternité Mondiale*, 1953).

Teaching History (London: Ministry of Education 1953).

The Teaching of History in Germany (Bulletin of the University of Liverpool Institute of Education, No. 4, Oct. 1953).

Rencontres franco-allemands d'historiens, 1950–1953 (Mayence: Direction générale des affaires culturelles, 1954: see above, Eckert, G., *Deutschland-Frankreich-Europa*).

History Without Bias? (London: The Council of Christians and Jews, 1954).

Histoire et Enseignement (Bulletin de la Féderation Belge des Professeurs d'histoire, 1954).

Recommandations aux auteurs et aux éditeurs sur l'histoire de Belgique (*ibid.*).

Impartial History (London: *The Times*, 16 Sept. 1954).

Chaudhury, K. P.: *The Content of History in Indian Schools* (Delhi, Ministry of Education, 1954).

Schüddekopf, O.-E.: *Die Internationale Schulbucharbeit* (*Aussen-politik*, Nov. 1955).

Wilson, H. E. & F. H.: *International Study of History Textbooks* (*Fraternité Mondiale* 1955).

Puttemans, A.: *L'enseignement de l'histoire et la révision des manuels scolaires en vue d'une meilleure compréhension Internationale* (Brussels, Imprimerie des Sciences, 1955).

Syllabus Bénélux (Fédération Belge des Professeurs d'Histoire: Brussels 1956).

Melzi, d'Eril F.: *La Comprensione tra Oriente ed Occidente nell'insegnamento storiografico* (Scuola e Cultura, Marzo 1957).

L'Europe et l'Ecole (Centre européen de la Culture, Geneva, April 1957).

Travaux et Résultats de la Révision des Manuels d'Histoire (*Courrier de l'Education Nationale*, Luxembourg Ministry of Education, Oct. 1957).

Geschichte in Wissenschaft und Unterricht (Stuttgart, Verlag E. Klett; various dates).

Shiksha (*Journal of the Education Department*, United Provinces, India; Lucknow, various dates, 1953–7).

Narotchnitsky, A. L.: *General Principles of Textbooks on History and of Teaching the History of the U.S.S.R., of West-European Countries, and of Americas in the Schools of the U.S.S.R.* (presented to the UNESCO East/West Conference at Tokyo, 22 Sept.–4 Oct. 1958).

Pulman, Olga: *Les Manuels d'Histoire en U.R.S.S.* (Bruxelles, Fédération belge des Professeurs d'Histoire, 1959).

VIII.　GENERAL BOOKS

Lin Shao-Yang: *A Chinese Appeal to Christendom* (Watts 1911).

Toynbee, A.: *A Study of History* (Oxford University Press 1934ff.)

Toynbee, A.: *The World and the West* (Oxford University Press 1953).

Moreland and Chatterji: *A Short History of India* (Longmans 1936).

Garratt, G. T. (ed.): *The Legacy of India* (Oxford University Press 1937).

Grousset, R.: *Histoire de la Chine* (Paris: Fayard 1942).

Grousset, R.: *Bilan de l'histoire* (Paris: Plon 1946).

Arbery, J.: *British Orientalists* (Collins 1943).

Nehru, J.: *The Discovery of India* (Meridian Books 1946).

Weber, A.: *Farewell to European History* (Kegan Paul 1947).

Rifaat Bey, M.: *The Awakening of Modern Egypt* (Longmans 1947).

Samuel and Thomas: *Education and Society in Modern Germany* (Routledge & Kegan Paul 1949).

Halecki, O.: *The Limits and Divisions of European History* (Sheed and Ward 1950).

Atabinien, Rechid Safvet: *Les Apports Turcs dans le Peuplement et la Civilisation de l'Europe Orientale* (Istanbul: Cituris Frères 1952).

Winter, H. J. J.: *Eastern Science* (Murray 1952).

Needham, J.: *Science and Civilisation in China, Vols.* 1 *and* 2 (Cambridge University Press 1954 and 1956).

Sinor, Denis (ed.): *Orientalism and History* (Cambridge: Heffer 1954).

Pulleyblank, E. G.: *Chinese History and World History* (Cambridge University Press, n.d.: ?1955).

Barraclough, G.: *History in a Changing World* (Oxford: Blackwell 1955).

Index